INTERNET CULTURE in easy steps

Josh Smith

In easy steps is an imprint of Computer Step
Southfield Road . Southam
Warwickshire CV33 OFB . England

Tel: 01926 817999 Fax: 01926 817005
http://www.computerstep.com

Notice of Liability

Every effort has been made to ensure that this book contains accurate and current information. However, Computer Step and the author shall not be liable for any loss or damage suffered by readers as a result of any information contained herein.

Trademarks

All trademarks are acknowledged as belonging to their respective companies.

Printed and bound in the United Kingdom

ISBN 1-84078-018-5

Contents

Chapter One

The Internet Unravelled

In this chapter, you will learn about the various aspects and facets of the Internet, so that you will be able to understand the concepts discussed in the rest of the book.

Covers

Introduction

Within the last few years, the term 'the Internet' has slipped into everyday language, invading our newspapers, magazines and even our TV sets. Loosely defined, the Internet is an international computer network – or rather, a network of networks – at the heart of which lies a number of powerful and permanently linked computers. To join the Internet, you connect your computer to any of these computers, and are then able to talk to, and disseminate information to, every other computer on the Internet.

The Internet, then, offers a means of communicating in a profoundly different way to other more conventional media. However, a major problem for this global network of information is misinformation: the Internet is many different things to different people. Technical boffins might have you believe that it's all to do with packets, processes and protocols. A business executive would tell you of the great unexploited commercial possibilities that the Internet offers, while the popular media informs us that the Internet is corrupting our nation's youth, and that its lack of regulation will destroy the fabric of our society. Indeed, all these opinions have elements of truth within them.

This book isn't designed to teach you how to use the Internet, with regard to its technical elements. For this, see Internet UK, also in the 'in easy steps' series.

Few, though, would consider the local supermarket to be the most important facet of life, nor the top shelf of a newsagent's newsrack. The Internet, put simply, is about people, and as such has developed a culture of its own – a members' code of online conduct for interaction, and a collection of ideas and habits which are learned, shared and passed on to new members.

It is this book's aim to offer you practical advice in understanding all the *human aspects* of the Internet, and to show that the question of 'why' people do things is just as important as 'how' they are done.

Getting Started

On this page I'm going to try and explain in 300 words what most books dwell on with 30,000.

If you want to use the Internet for e-mail and IRC (Internet Relay Chat) only, there are a wide variety of computer 'platforms' you can use – PCs (386 and above), older Macs, Amigas, Acorns, and even Ataris.

If you really want to make the best of your online experience (ie, full web functionality, connections which aren't painfully slow, and technical support which is of real use to you) you are going to need a 'proper' computer.

This may not endear me to computer enthusiasts of an antique persuasion, yet the problem is not only a lack of computing power, but one of software availability. To run these programs you will need at least a 486 PC or a decent Power Mac.

You will also need a modem. 33.6k modems are very cheap and it's not worth skimping the extra tenner on a 14.4k model which is significantly slower. 56k models are also available, although they don't offer a great improvement in speed, the limiting factor being the quality of the telephone network rather than the modem.

In addition to this you will need an account with an ISP – Internet Service Provider. There are hundreds to choose from – eg, Demon, BT Internet and Virgin Net.

There are also a number of OSPs – Online Service Providers, who typically provide not only access to the Internet, but content available only to their members. Some of the most popular in the UK are AOL (America Online), CompuServe (who are now owned by AOL), BT Lineone and MSN. They generally charge by the hour after a complimentary five hours per month. If you spend more than two or three hours a week online these can become prohibitively expensive.

World Wide Web

The World Wide Web is probably the largest method of information dispersal on the Internet today.

HANDY TIP **The World Wide Web can be abbreviated to WWW, or just 'the Web'.**

To weave the Web you need a 'web browser'. Several different companies have produced these, but two products have proved to be predominant:

- Microsoft Internet Explorer, and;
- Netscape Navigator.

Microsoft Internet Explorer

Microsoft was rather late to the fray, but after it achieved its goal of conquering the desktop market, it turned its attention to the growing need for Internet products.

At the time of writing, Internet Explorer has approximately 40% of the browser market, although this is likely to increase now that the product is completely integrated into Windows 98. Internet Explorer is available to download from *http://www.microsoft.com/*

A product that is 'freeware' does not need to be paid for. This differs from 'shareware' products which allow you a free trial for a specified period of time.

Netscape Navigator

The first graphical browser was called NCSA Mosaic, and quickly grew in popularity. Several programmers left NCSA and formed Netscape, and its dominance was largely uncontested until Microsoft took the plunge into the digital ocean of the World Wide Web.

Currently, Navigator and its packaged version (known as Netscape Communicator) is still the most popular Web browser, and its decision to be designated freeware is designed to ensure this. Few ISPs (Internet Service Providers) and computer manufacturers will install Netscape Navigator as the default browser. It remains many people's favourite, but realistically there is little difference between the two browsers. Netscape Navigator is available to download from *http://home.netscape.com/*

The Web Browser interface

Here is what all the various 'bits 'n' bobs' of a browser's interface do.

HANDY TIP

You can identify a WWW address by its 'http://' prefix. HTTP is HyperText Transfer Protocol, the method by which the web page data is transmitted.

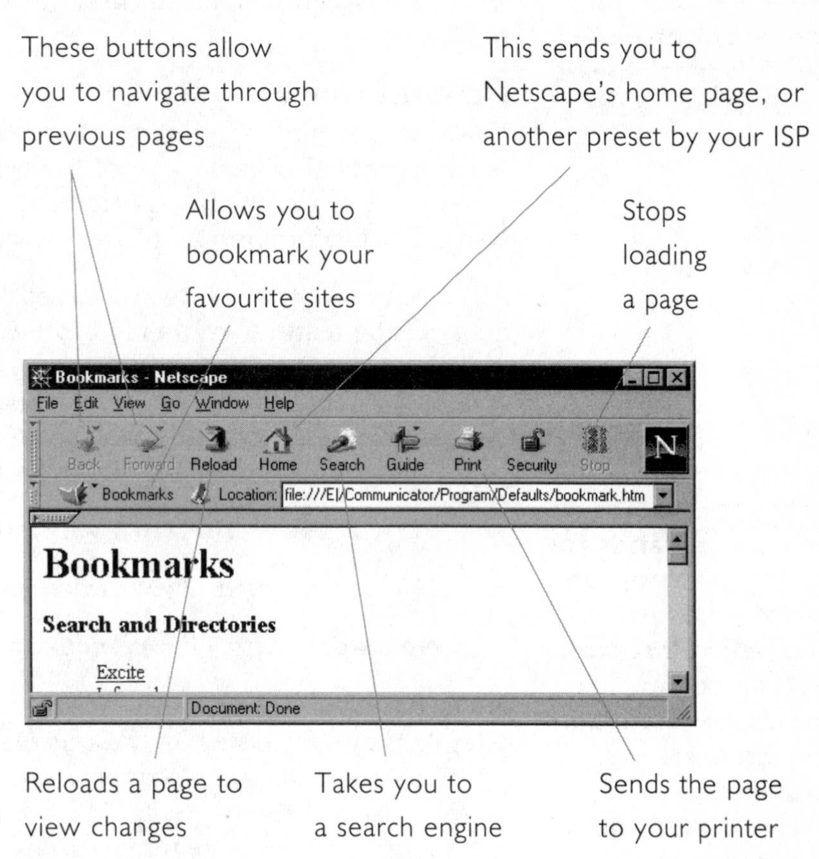

Search Engines

'Meta tags' are unseen bits of data which tell search engines what the page is all about.

So what is required to weave your way through this virtual spider's den? What you need is a search site. These sites operate 'bots' which 'crawl' around the WWW searching for information stored in 'meta tags' and categorise the work based on these and the content of the page. The different way in which sites accomplish this means that they will all produce different results, but many are very comprehensive and reflect the true variety of the Web with over three million records. (*http://www.yahoo.com/* is the most popular search site.)

The Users' Network

The Users' Network is known by several different names – eg, 'Usenet', 'news' and 'newsgroups'.

Unlike the World Wide Web, the Users' Network, or Usenet for short, has received very little coverage from the mass media. It is the Internet's premier debate forum, where users get to stand in their pulpits and set the world to rights.

Newsreaders

There are several different newsreaders available, with Forte Agent being easily one of the best. It is not perhaps as intuitive or simplistic as Microsoft News or Netscape News, but it offers much greater functionality.

A free version of the software, called Free Agent, retains many of the features of its big brother and is readily available from the Forte site. Otherwise, the registered version (which costs about £20 without the manuals) comes with a facility that enables you to collect and sort your e-mail (an uninspiring but essential feature).

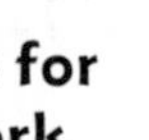

NNTP stands for Network News Transfer Protocol. NNTP servers are news servers from which users can download newsgroups and update their content.

- Forte Agent – *http://www.forteinc.com/*
- Microsoft – *http://www.microsoft.com/*
- Netscape – *http://home.netscape.com/*

Newsgroups

There are over 25,000 newsgroups on public NNTP servers (Network News Transfer Protocol – see HANDY TIP in the margin) around the world as well as many more establishment, ISP or regional groups, which have a smaller distribution. The groups are split into a hierarchy, which allows the user to find groups which are of interest. Although a topic may be dealt with in several different groups, there are often distinct differences in the approach which is taken to that subject.

A 'newbie' is a new user, who probably doesn't know a lot about the Internet.

To remedy this, many newsgroups have an FAQ (Frequently Asked Questions) file. Many new users read them first (or lurk in the group), to get a feel for what the subject matter is before posting a contribution of their own.

Let us take, for example, the newsgroup *alt.fan.asprin.* Its FAQ file clearly states that *'this group is not for discussion of the drug aspirin, nor any other pharmaceutical product'.* Yet every week that goes by, some careless chemist decides to ask something completely irrelevant.

Listed below are the most common top-level newsgroup hierarchies:

*alt.**	Anarchists, lunatics and terrorists, this category holds 'alternative' newsgroups – the 'dustbin' of Usenet.
*biz.**	Business related groups.
*comp.**	Computer related discussion groups.
*news.**	Usenet issues – discussion groups relating to how Usenet itself operates.
*rec.**	Recreational, hobbies and leisure groups.
*sci.**	Science specific subjects are discussed here.
*soc.**	Groups concerned with social issues
*talk.**	Serious debating groups (usually politics, religion and other controversial subjects).
*uk.**	UK specific groups, taken by all servers within the UK.

Netiquette

This is an issue central to the use of Usenet as a debating medium. The length of signatures (files placed at the end of each article you post) and the language used is important to understand if you are to be accepted into the Usenet community.

There are no rules within Usenet, but there are many guidelines you are expected to follow. It does also depend on the spirit and ethos of the individual group. This subject is discussed in much greater depth in Chapters Five and Seven.

Electronic Mail

Electronic Mail is perhaps one of the most practical and useful aspects of the Internet. It has three advantages over more traditional forms of communication:

- It's very cheap – sending a message takes only a few seconds at the cost of a local rate telephone call.
- It's also very quick (often as fast, although perhaps not as instantaneous, as a telephone call).
- Information is transferred in digital form, so it allows data to be communicated graphically and accurately. It also saves time otherwise spent re-inputting documents.

You can easily recognise an e-mail address because it has an '@' sign in the middle – for example: *user@host.com*

An E-mail Client

'Attachments' allows you to send formatted text or digitised images using e-mail

Designates a subject that will be identifiable to the recipient(s)

The 'To:' field allows you to specify recipients

The 'Cc:' field means you can send copies to interested parties

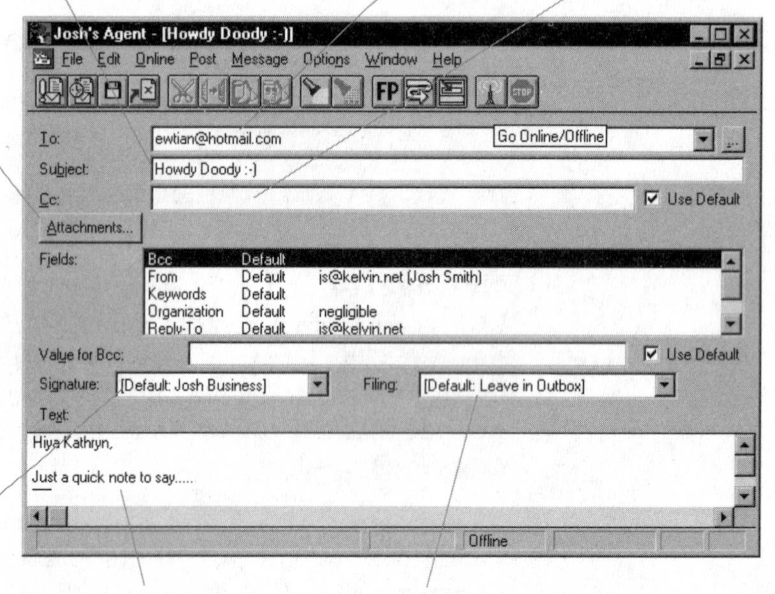

Like Usenet posts, you can attach signatures to e-mails

Main body of text

A filing system allows you to organise incoming and outgoing mails

Data entry 'fields' allow you to enter details (eg, address) whilst 'headers' tell you which data to input.

Unsolicited Commercial E-mail

UCE (Unsolicited Commercial E-mail) is a growing problem on the Internet. E-mail addresses are harvested from web pages and particularly from Usenet posts (where it is considered impolite not to give readers some method of contacting you), and users are soon bombarded with junk mail and scams.

However many users 'munge' their e-mail address to confuse e-mail harvesters. Take for example my address: *js@computerstep.com*. I might change my reply address to *js@spamblock.computerstep.com*. Most users would know to remove the *'spamblock'* from the address, but many automated e-mail robots do not. For further details on avoiding spam, see 'Spam' in Chapter Ten.

Mailing Lists

Mailing lists are similar to Usenet newsgroups, but they are easier to set up and, in the days of old, were available to those who did not have access to a news server.

For many users, it is rather inconvenient to have their mailbox flooded with lists which may deliver up to 50 or 60 articles per day. It is useful to have e-mail software with good filtering facilities. Both Forte's Agent (the registered version) and Eudora Pro offer this service:

- Eudora Pro – *http://www.qualcomm.com/*
- Forte Agent – *http://www.forteinc.com/*

Microsoft and Netscape also bundle e-mail clients with their web browser suites. Microsoft Outlook is just such a program, often used by new Internet users. It is a newsreader-cum-e-mail client-cum-contact organiser. Some would argue that it does none of these jobs very well, but if you want to have a look at these products, point your browser towards:

- Microsoft Outlook – *http://www.microsoft.com/*
- Netscape Mail – *http://www.netscape.com/*

Internet Relay Chat

IRC (Internet Relay Chat) is probably the most 'cultured' of any method of communication on the Internet. There is an important distinction between real-time forums like IRC, and delayed response communication devices such as e-mail and Usenet. (This is discussed in detail in Chapters Four and Five respectively.)

To use IRC you need a client. There are several different offerings which are designed to help you weave your way across the cyber-patois.

- mIRC – *http://www.mirc.co.uk/*
- PIRCH – *http://www.pirch.com/*
- Ircle – *http://www.ircle.com/*

The first two are for PC adherents, while the last is for Macintosh zealots. 'mIRC' is the most popular, although PIRCH is bit richer on features (and gimmicks). They're shareware, so if you use them, and you like them, then you are required to register them too.

REMEMBER

A server is something which is (usually) permanently connected to the Internet and allows clients to connect to them, to upload (ie, send) or download (ie, receive) data of some sort.

How IRC works

It is a bit of a complex beastie this, but in simple terms it goes something like this. Someone who owns a server sets up the IRC server program on it (it's called an ircd) and lets people connect to it. Once connected to the server, people form channels. The first person to join a channel automatically becomes a channel operator (someone who controls the channel) and a founder (if the server has 'services' and supports 'channel registration').

Usually people start to congregate in certain channels, because although being a 'chop' (channel operator) is all fine and dandy, it isn't much fun if you haven't got anyone to talk to. Existing 'chops' can appoint new channel operators if they choose, to help them run the channel.

IRC Networks

Often, servers will link together to form networks. The advantage of this is that a server in California will be quite a distance, even in electronic terms, from someone in Britain. If a British server was to link to a Californian server, the British could then use the UK server while the Californians (who you just can't seem to avoid on IRC) could attach to their Californian server and the two servers could talk to each other.

'Lag' is the name given to the response time of a server (or other users) in relation to you. Anything over 10 seconds makes conversation painfully slow. A 'Netsplit' occurs when a server loses communication with other servers on the network. This is the usual reason why people suddenly disappear from a channel.

HANDY TIP

'Services' allow users to register channels and nicknames (a handle which identifies you on IRC) so that you can maintain ownership of them even when you are offline.

There are four major IRC networks, and hundreds of smaller ones. The main ones are:

- Dalnet – *defiant.uk.eu.dal.net*
- EfNet – *efnet.demon.co.uk*
- Undernet – *london.uk.eu.undernet.org*
- IRCNet – *ircnet.demon.co.uk*

The main distinction between them is that Dalnet and Undernet have 'services' whilst Efnet and IRCNet (which is a European split of Efnet) do not.

Both have their merits and demerits. Efnet and IRCNet are a bit anarchical, but on the Internet you often find that a lack of control is no bad thing.

Conversely, Dalnet and Undernet are often very 'laggy' (slow), because the services put a great deal of strain on the network. Try all of them, but eventually the one which you visit most won't depend on the network, rather on the channels (and users) which it holds.

Net Games

There is one advantage to playing games on the Internet: you can never 'complete' them, so you can play for as long as you want. Whether your recreational tastes are towards blowing three-eyed digerati to bits in Doom or pretending to be a bald-headed French captain, it is out there, somewhere.

E-mail games

These are included for the sake of posterity. Many people think they are boring, but you might find one that appeals to you. Decent chess players are able to play games via e-mail, but you do need to have a good knowledge of chess notation to do this. If you have access to a newsreader (and can work out what all the buttons do) then have a look at the *rec.games.chess* newsgroups.

Netrek

Ah ha, now this game is really neat! It's loosely based on Star Trek. You can play a team game (with up to 8 players on each side) and in a variety of different ships you get to fly around, blowing 'baddies' up and bombing planets.

A 'Twink' is a name given to someone who isn't very good at Netrek.

There are two 'aspects' to the game. Firstly, there is the tactical element. This means that the first time you play, when you engage the enemy in a 'dogfight' you get blown up and they fly away unscathed. Then there is the 'strategic' element – who to attack, where to attack, when. It may not be immediately apparent what this involves, but when one of your team-mates starts shouting 'Twink! – What did you do that for?' when you bomb a planet he is about to take, you will soon understand.

Okay, so it sounds a bit nerdy, but it is a game with a kind of depth that you don't see in commercially produced software. However, it does take quite a bit of getting into, and it's easy to ring up a substantial phone bill while you're flying your way across the stars. For more information take a look at 'The Netrek Continuum' – *http://www.netrek.org/*.

Online Doom and Quake

These are quite fun as well – but not that I admit to taking delight in blowing my fellow netizens into byte-sized chunks, being the devout pacifist that I am!

Moving along from the tiresome puns, these games are considerably more fun online and great for educating some modem-less bods, who think they're God with a bazooka.

You will usually need a registered copy of the respective software and find a server which is, on the grand digital scale of things, close to you. If you are 'lagged' you will be at a severe disadvantage to your opponent.

Many ISP employees enjoy Doom and Quake and have the advantage of a 100mb/s link to the server and 'ping' times in the range of mere milliseconds. (For more on 'pings', see 'Lag' in Chapter Four.)

If you are any good you can join a 'clan'. You can then play matches against other 'clans' and turn simple murder into mass homicide. Marvellous.

MultiUser Dungeons

MUDs, MOOs or MU*s (as they are collectively known) were one of the first games to be played across the primaeval Internet. If you ever had an old ZX Spectrum or Commodore 64 you surely will be familiar with the 'you stand outside a castle...go North to...', type of text-based RPG games that seemed so great then, and that just seem so archaic now.

Well MUDs were a bit like that, except they were more complicated. People don't play them much now, and they aren't that easy to get to grips with. To play them you need a Telnet client (a slightly disfunctional, all expense spared one is included with Windows) and a lot of patience.

They are quite fun and if you meet any Net old timers, they'll probably reminisce about their favourite MUD. (At least now you won't be surprised that there isn't a rhino horn in the middle of their head or that they don't live on a health farm.)

- MUD FAQ – *http://www.lysator.liu.se/mud/faq/faq1.html*

The WELL

Stewart Brand and Larry Brilliant founded the Whole Earth 'Lectronic Link in 1985, starting with a dialogue between the fiercely creative and independent writers and readers of the Whole Earth Review.

The WELL home site's blurb about its service describes the WELL as a giant coffee house (this is a good analogy in many respects: if you think of those really posh cafes in London, where the coffee doesn't taste too good and is expensive, but it's a really hip meeting place, where famous people hang out). Well, (if you excuse the pun) the WELL is a bit like that. The Web access version of the account costs $10 a month (about £7) and is clumsier, and indeed harder to use than a Usenet newsreader. A $15 a month account called a 'WELL.com' account is also available which lets you use 'picospan', the proprietary software, which although decidedly better than using your trusty web browser to muddle through the topics, it isn't exactly great.

What really makes the WELL popular is the type of people who use it. They tend to be (particularly in the literary conferences) better 'connected' and have a much sounder background of experience than most of the participants of similar groups on Usenet.

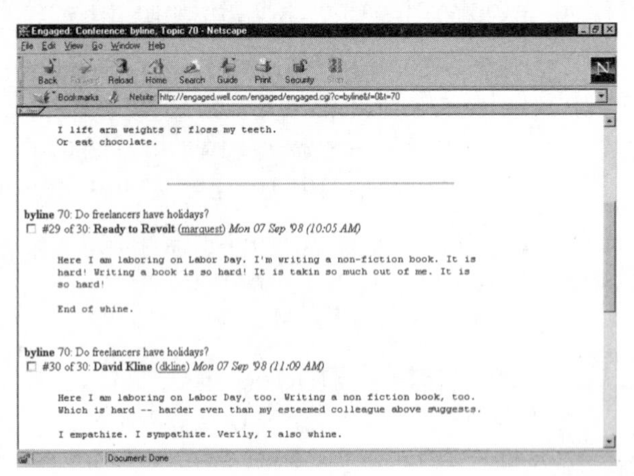

There are over 260 conferences on the WELL, so there is bound to be something that will take your fancy, but unless you i) don't have a job or ii) don't have a life, you will find it difficult to keep up with more than one or two of them.

The WELL is in fact only a very small part of the Net, but most of its users think it is the most important.

Chapter Two

The Changing Internet

The Internet has changed a great deal since its inception in 1967. In some ways this has been for the better, in others it has not. Despite this, what the Internet *was* tells us a lot about what the Internet *is*, 30 years later.

Covers

History of the Internet

The Internet is very different from its predecessor, 40 years ago. The concept of a global network may not have been hatched in Microsoft's war rooms, but it did play a part in a previous contest for world domination.

In 1957, at the height of the Cold War, the Russians had just launched Sputnik, and in response the US Ministry of Defence formed ARPA, the Advanced Research Projects Agency to 'up' the rate of its own technological advancement. Twelve years later, in 1969, this formed ARPANet – a project to develop the world's first military research network, or specifically the world's first decentralised computer network.

The online bomb shelter

In these days of old, no-one had PCs! The IT experience, up until the 1970s, consisted of mainframe computers and dumb terminals. The terminals took the user's input and sent it to a very large and very expensive mainframe, which processed it. It then spewed out an answer and sent it back to the terminal.

These costly systems were, initially, only available to the military, academia and very large companies. Particularly within the academic and the military world there was a great desire to share information between research units and defence contractors.

A 'node' is a general term for any single station on a network.

With the possibility of nuclear bombardment, particularly of military research facilities, the structural integrity of any wide area network was considered particularly important.

In a traditional setup, either a loop or star-based network configuration was used. The disadvantage with these systems is that if any node (in the former configuration) or the central node (in the latter setup) were to be damaged, then the ability of the network to function would be severely impaired.

The concept of a decentralised network is that there are several ways to get to the same place. This represents two important improvements on the traditional setup: firstly, if a few nodes are damaged by sabotage or aerial attack (as was feared for the duration of the Cold War) then the network could still function adequately. Secondly, it means that in electronic terms at least, no node is particularly distant from any other node.

A protocol is an agreed method by which a system operation is to take place. It is particularly important for exchanging data between computers. They may be very different in configuration, but providing they use the same 'protocol' the information transfer should be successful.

The TCP/IP story

In 1973, the renamed US Defence Advanced Research Projects Agency (DARPA) instigated a research programme to investigate techniques and technologies for communicating information across decentralised networks. This was called the 'Internetting project' and resulted in the name we use to describe the global network of today, the 'Internet'.

Two separate protocols, TCP and IP, were developed: Transmission Control Protocol, and Internet Protocol. Thus, TCP/IP (which you'll hear a lot of Internet users talk about) is not one protocol, but a *protocol suite.*

Related Networks

In 1980, two other networking projects, BITNET and CSNET were begun. BITNET was another primarily academic network which provided some unique services including LISTSERV, a mailing list system, which is still used.

Nowadays, BITNET is practically dead along with its parallel network in Europe (EARN.) Despite its slow decline during the early 1990s, much of what people associate with the Internet today was first spawned on BITNET, 15 years before.

In 1987, CSNET and BITNET combined to form the Corporation for Research and Education Networking (CREN). Although CSNET service was discontinued in 1991, it is interesting to note that the cost of the service was fully met by its participating members.

Giving Some Backbone

In 1986, the US National Science Foundation made their contribution to the Net, by initiating NSFNet, which up until recent years provided the main backbone (the large pipes which carry information between smaller groups of nodes) for the Internet. With up to 45 megabit per second facilities, it carried 12 billion packets per month between the networks it linked.

At a similar time, networks in Europe began to take root with JANET (Joint Academic Network) in the UK and NORDUNET in Scandinavia. Commercial service providers in Europe and the US also started to offer Internet connection for larger companies.

In a technological sense, NFSNet was not a huge progression, but you have to understand that prior to 1986, academics as such were not admitted to the 'Internet club'.

HANDY TIP

HTML, in its most basic form, was a language which enabled you to format text (bold, italics, etc) as well as give it certain properties, such as hyperlinking. In a more advanced form it is the lingua franca of the modern WWW. Take a look at HTML, also in the 'in easy steps' series.

Towards the end of the 80s, plans were made to shut down the old ARPANet pipes. There was a lot of concern over what effect this 54kbps (roughly equivalent to a quick modem today) line being pulled would have upon the proto-Internet. If you weren't in the room at the time (in 1990) you wouldn't have noticed!

NFSNet was an antithesis to the exclusivity of ARPANet and carried a historically radical philosophy. Much of the 'free speech' culture that exists on the Internet today is a result of the attitudes of NFSNet's initial users.

World Wide Web

To many people who have jumped on this digital bandwagon, the Internet *is* the World Wide Web – which it isn't. The scripting language behind the Web was invented by Tim Berners-Lee at CERN (European Nuclear Research Institute), Switzerland in 1989. Primarily its aim was to facilitate the sharing of high particle physics research amongst interested parties.

HTML (HyperText Markup Language), as it was, didn't support pictures, so the graphical functionality that is felt

'Hyperlinks' enable you to click on a word or picture in one document which will then take you to another, related document.

to be so important today didn't even exist then (which isn't surprising since most people didn't have a fast enough connection to deal with graphics). Its most useful aspect was the ability to string documents together through the use of hyperlinks. At the time it was another little insignificant backwater on the Internet – another 'interesting thing'.

In 1993, the University of Illinois developed a graphical interface to the Web, which they called Mosaic. Initially, it was only available for Xwindows, which is a graphical front-end to the UNIX operating system (in the same way that Windows 3.1 is a front-end to DOS, although Unixers would probably think the analogy a little demeaning).

With the next year the code was 'ported' (transferred) to Windows 3.1 and it was some of the developers of the original NCSA Mosaic that went off to found Netscape, who now have a 40% share of the huge browser market.

Usenet

'NetNews' as it was then known was born in 1979 when Tom Truscott and Jim Ellis, graduate students at Duke University, conceived of creating a discussion network for those within the UNIX community. In much the same way as NFSNet, Usenet was a reaction to the exclusion of academia from ARPANet. Although eventually it became available to ARPANet nodes, its users were treated as second class citizens.

UNIX is an operating system just like MS-DOS, except that it was developed much earlier and many of the conventions which it employs are still used on the Internet today.

As a result, the ethos of Usenet is still very much one of free speech and revolves around a lack of central control. In their handout proposing the idea, the graduates said,

"The goal of USENET has been to give every UNIX system the opportunity to join and benefit from a computer network (a poor man's ARPANet if you will.....)"

Internet Relay Chat

The IRC project was a development of a primitive UNIX program called 'talk'. It was based on existing real time conversation applications, and the original IRC client and server were written by Jarkko Oikarinen at the University of Oulu, Finland, in 1988.

IRC was first tested on a single machine with less than 20 users participating. It was then run on a suite of three computers, in Southern Finland, to establish its network capabilities.

Once tested, it quickly gained strength within FUNET (the Finnish national network) and soon spread to NORDUNET. By 1990, IRC had been popularised on the Internet proper.

Over five years later, specialised clients such as mIRC and PIRCH were developed. Most users still use IRCII, the traditional vanilla flavoured UNIX variant.

So, that's it. Historically you can mark the birth of the Internet from either 1957, 1969, 1979, 1983, 1988 or early 1994. For many people, the Net is only 4 years old and although a lot has happened in terms of the scale of the Internet, there haven't been any great technological developments in these last four years. This may come as somewhat of a surprise, but to quote Jack Rickard in 1995: 'the party has only just started!'

Data Communications

Bandwidth is a measurement of the amount of data that can be transferred from one node to another node. It is a specific term and varies depending on where the data is travelling to and from. It can also be used generally to describe the capacity of a network (or the Internet as a whole) to shunt information about, but this is not its original meaning.

Usage of the Internet has grown exponentially over the last few years – a dramatic growth in terms of users, an incomprehensible growth in terms of the information transmitted.

To deal with this mass explosion the Internet has had to adapt, and the technologies behind it develop. Usenet, which in the last two years has grown in terms of bandwidth usage by 997%, now exchanges twenty-two gigabytes a day between news servers.

Bits 'n' bytes

This needs a little explanation. With data transmission there are two main issues: the amount of data that *is* being transferred and that amount of data which *can* be transferred. To clarify, just because a pipe *can* transfer 45mb/s doesn't mean it does it all the time.

You can use the Internet for years without knowing how this all works, as it is hidden behind a veil of winsocks, pretty pictures and icons. This is rather fortunate since the whole business can be more than a little confusing.

Data is either measured in *bytes* or in *bits*. A bit is one binary digit – thus it is either an 'on' signal or an 'off' signal, a '1' or a '0'. Most computer books have funny pictures of light bulbs to explain this, but I wouldn't be so insulting – I can't draw light bulbs anyway.

There are 8 bits in a byte. Why is this? Did Babbage only have 8 fingers? No. This is because in the days of old, when men could afford season tickets and computer programmers couldn't draw pretty pictures, it was a rather textual experience.

The predominant text format was called 'ASCII' and had a 128 character 'alphabet' with numbers, letters and 'control characters' (among which were things like carriage returns and pound signs and all the other gubbins you find on your keyboard, plus a little bit more).

'Binary', for mathematically minded people, is called mode 2 because there are two modes (clever huh?) – it's either on or it's off. 2^7 (or 2 x 2 x 2 x 2 x 2 x 2 x 2) is 128. So with seven binary digits there are 128 possible permutations. The other digit is put to other uses, notably error checking.

With a 33.6kb/s modem, the *'kbps'* stands for *kilobits* per second – *kilo* being a thousand, *mega* being a million, and *giga* being a thousand million (and for the sake of trivia, a million million is a *tera).*

When we talk about the size of a file we generally talk in terms of *bytes,* because originally all files were text based so you knew that if a file was 200 bytes long it had about 200 letters in it, give or take a few control characters.

Now, this is absolute proof that computer scientists love to make things complicated. A 1kb file, where *Kb* stands for kilobytes, isn't 1000 bytes long, it's 1024. Marvellous. It's all to do with those lovely powers again, but suffice to say that a 14.4kb/s modem won't take a second to transfer a 14.4kb file. It will take eight seconds plus a little bit, if you excuse the pun.

Speed of data transmission is measured in *bits,* whilst the amount of data is measured in *bytes.*

Now I bet you think that you really didn't need to know that, but you do! Rather than a digression to show you just how ridiculous the Internet can be, it is really irritating when you log on to download something for an hour and it takes eight.

Is it that simple? Nay, nay! It's one of the first things you learn about technology, and Internet technology in particular, that nothing can be *that* simple.

Modem speeds

Let us assume for a moment that you have a 56kb/s modem. There are a few things you need to bear in mind. Firstly you probably won't have a 56kb/s connection unless you live in a flat above your ISP; more likely that you'll get a 40–45kb/s connection, give or take a few thousand bits, due to line interference and signal degradation.

Compression

Compression is also an issue, but that is a whole new can of worms. Compression works by taking a series of similar information and expressing it in a shorter form. Taking a 'bitmap' picture for example with a lot of sky, instead of expressing a section of it as BLUE-BLUE-BLUE-BLUE it could just say 4-BLUE.

It is for this reason that compression varies. With a traditional landscape a lot of the colours are the same so the compression is very high, but the *compression ratio* will vary from file to file, whether it is a picture file or a text file or any sort.

Many of the files on the Internet are already compressed in the form of *'zips'* which are identified by a *'.zip'* (or more rarely '.z', '.gz' or '.arj' with different compressors) at the end of their file names. The program used to do this, PKZIP, is readily available and an essential tool for any wannabe netizen.

Modems also compress data using a standard called v.42bis which can increase speeds quite considerably – usually up to a limit of 115,200kb/s. v.42 is not as effective a compression system as the one which PKZIP employs, but it is *on the fly* which means compressing and decompressing data quickly is very easy.

The point? Well, if a file is already compressed then the modem's own compression isn't going to help one little bit (another dreadful pun). This means that the time taken to download a file will depend not only on how well the file has been 'squished', but whether it has already been 'squished'.

Bottlenecks

Bottlenecks are one other concept that it is important to get to grips with. The rule is that the speed of data transmission is only as fast as its slowest link. If you have a 33.6kb/s link to your ISP and your ISP has a 45mb/s link to node A and node A has a 10kb/s link to node B, your destination, then the maximum possible speed of that transfer will be 10kb/s, assuming of course that no-one else is using the same lines simultaneously. Another avid downloader jumping onto that 10kb/s pipe can really slow things up – to quote Douglas Adams, the greatest hitchhiker of them all, 'your mileage may vary'.

Bandwidth baddies

On the Internet, all bandwidth is a precious commodity, since it only takes one important section of a network to grind to a digital halt to turn the whole thing into the online equivalent of the M25 at 8am in the morning. Slow, frustrating, boring, but rest assured, people won't desist from tooting their horns.

The most flagrant of bandwidth consumers are graphically laden web sites and Usenet. Demon, the UK's largest ISP to date, receives 22gb of Usenet material a day on its full feed. When you consider that there are 100,000 news servers on the Internet, it is pretty incredible.

Approximately, 35% of all Usenet posts are spam whilst another 30% are 'cancels' for spam, which stop the annoying little messages being downloaded by people from the news server. They don't actually delete the spams so the problem remains.

A large proportion, in size terms at least, of spam and non-spam posts are binaries. As opposed to a normal text based posting (5k at most) these pictures or programs may be 200k or 300k long. Usenet is a very poor medium for shunting big files around, since it sends them indiscriminately, whether they are really wanted or not.

Graphic laden web sites aren't just annoying for users, who spend ages tapping their fingers waiting for the wretched pictures to appear, but for people who have to use the same 'pipes' to exchange data across.

The secret to using the Internet, for now at least, is patience. It's much cheaper than a super-duper modem and much more effective too.

Censorship and Ownership

Free Speech is one of the Internet's 'sacred cows', but as our history of the Net shows, this has not always been the case. I think it is true to say that people don't value things that they take for granted, and thus many users don't appreciate the importance of free debate.

Essential to this lack of regulation is a lack of ownership. This is a bit of a misnomer, however. People and companies do own the Internet, but they own very little bits of it. For example, some people own IRC servers, some own news servers, some own the pipes which carry the data and most consumers support the Internet by paying their ten quid a month to their ISP (Internet Service Provider).

The joy is that if someone pulls the plug on their news server or digs up their pipes, then the effect is minimal since the Internet is a decentralised network and routes around bad nodes.

Government legislation

On the UK front at least, there has been little government intervention over the transmission of material across the Internet, mainly as a result of the poor reception of such legislation in other countries.

The US government's first attempt at censorship came from the Senator for Nebraska, Jim Exon, after he saw a programme on NBC (a US news channel) about how the Internet was a breeding ground for paedophilia and other pornography.

In July 1995, the Senate passed the Communications Decency Act which allowed fines up to $100,000 and two years in prison to be levied against those contrary to the Act. Internet access providers would also be held liable for offensive material on their servers posted by users.

Although the Act was later rejected as being unconstitutional and conflicting with the First Amendment (which relates to Free Speech) it was an important landmark case in Internet history.

The US was not the only country involved in the censorship debacle. France instructed all their ISPs to remove the whole of the *alt.** hierarchy from their news servers, although their concern was more with subversives such as satellite cryptography codes and the like. The French clearly don't consider porn subversive.

The *'alt'* groups do contain most of the binary (picture) material carried by Usenet, the large majority of which is of an erotic nature. Their removal did little to prevent the access of such material by interested parties, since it was still readily available over the World Wide Web and on IRC, but the principles behind it were of great interest to the Internet community.

Why is it so important?

The Internet is unique, in relation to other communication media, in that it is responsive and vast. Whereas with magazines or television the topic, level and coverage is decided by a broadcaster or an editor, with the Internet you get to choose or request the information you require. This is essential when you consider the depth and breadth this veritable lexicon of knowledge contains.

Discussion groups on the Internet provide a relatively unbiased opinion on issues, not because the people who post to the groups are unopinionated (indeed they are usually very opinionated) but because of the wide range of views which are presented.

With a 'controlled' medium like television, the view of the producer or the political orientation of the channel is usually influential in deciding which opinions take prominence, and which are presented less persuasively. On Usenet, no-one's pulpit is higher than anyone else's, although the ability to write persuasively is not shared by everyone. In this sense, the Internet is a substantial threat to traditional media – which perhaps goes some way to explaining why the media so often objects to its more liberal aspects.

Chapter Three

Textual Communication

For now at least, the Internet is primarily a text based medium in that all the opinions users express are communicated in written form. In this chapter we look at what you can learn about a person from not only 'what' they say, but 'how' they say it as well as delving into the depths of the online *lingua franca*.

Covers

Reading Between The Lines?

On the Internet you can't see the raised eyebrow, the furrowed brow, the wink or the grin. You can't hear the hearty chuckle, the tone of irony and the hum of anger. Indeed, communicating on the Internet demands that you be a very perceptive individual in many respects.

It's only words, and words are all I have, to take your heart away . . .

So what means do we have to convey the whole host of human emotion, that is so integrally part of the human condition? A piece of coffee stained, moulded plastic into which you can channel a vast array of emotions, laughter, joy, hate and anger and send them thousands of miles around the world.

Of course, many people think this is rather limiting, as though words alone just weren't quite good enough. They want pictures, full motion gubbins and sound. It seems curious to me that these things would be desirable, when not quite knowing who is on the other end is half the fun.

Is Jurassic Park a better form of art than Romeo and Juliet and should Shakespeare make way for Spielberg? I think not.

The fact is you can tell an awful lot about people from the way they write. You might not be able to ascertain whether they have blue eyes or brown eyes, blond hair or brown hair, but you can tell how they feel – which is surely more valuable information.

Online style

The main reason why online writing is so different in structure to that offline is that there is a general trend on the Net to make your words sound as if they are being spoken rather than read, which inevitably leads to a considerable amount of colloquialism.

Conversely, although the actual words may be quite informal, the punctuation is often precise, reflecting the precision which is a necessary part of the average programmer's psyche.

The impetus to use correct English does depend on whether the users are newbies, who would likely use correct English, 'boy racing' (semi-experienced) users who seem to be completely devoid of all syntactical acumen, and the old timers who seem to be a tad fanatical about it.

It also depends on the situation. For example, colloquialisms and the absence of dots and dashes, commas and colons is much more acceptable in e-mail and IRC than it is on Usenet. On the WWW you are expected to write as though you would for publication (but given the work of some popular media journalists, I guess that doesn't set the standard unobtainably high).

How emphasis is given to words

When lacking the intonation of normal speech, many people online feel the need to identify which words have emphasis placed upon them.

To achieve this, some users emphasise words by placing them in capitals, although to many this is more akin to shouting than intonating, so is considered rather brutal. Another technique is to spread out the letters *L I K E T H I S* or enclose the phrase in asterisks, *like this*.

Of course, the use of these symbols has diversified over the course of time. For example, there is a semantic difference between *emphasis like this*, which makes the phrase more forceful as a whole, and *emphasis* *like* *this*, which suggests the author is speaking slowly as well.

Sometimes the asterisk characters are substituted for carets: *^^foo^^*, or signs of equality: *==foo==*, or even angle brackets: *<foo>*.

Other uses for our angular friends

More commonly, however, angle brackets are used to indicate expressions, moods, movements or sound effects.

<bang>, *<hic>*, *<ring>*, *<grin>*, *<kick>*, *<dang>* etc.

Angle brackets are also more rarely used to indicate a typical members of a larger class or group, eg:

So this <geek> goes up to a pelican crossing . . .

There is also a convention to represent vocal illiteracies – the text:

He really is a very charming fool^H^H^Hyoung man,

Rather obscurely, this reads: 'He really is a very charming fool, er, young man'.

Other peculiarities

You will notice that many Internet users tend to place punctuation outside rather than inside quotation marks (which follows the grammatical convention used when quotation marks indicate emphasis rather than direct speech):

In the run box type, 'c:\windows\system\command.com'.

rather than . . .

In the run box type, 'c:\windows\system\command.com.'

The reason for this is quite sensible. If you directly copy the material in the quotes and paste it onto a run box or a DOS prompt then it won't recognise the command, because of the erroneous period at the end of the line.

Technical tendencies

On a technical note, the limitations of the ASCII character set (most notably its lack of support for subscript and superscript characters) means that certain expressions, usually mathematical, have to be expressed in a different way. Given the scientific background of the Net this is not a new problem.

For example, a caret is used to express powers, whilst an asterisk implies a multiplication _(eg, 3*3 = 9_, but _3^3 = 27)._ This tradition with the caret originally dates from Algol-60 which used a similarly archaic ASCII character that later developed into the hat shaped figure used today.

You may also find some users express a power function as two asterisks (eg, *3**3 = 27)*. This derives from the programming language C, where this notation is used. For scientific notation the letter 'e' replaces 'x 10^x' so 1.6e5 is 1.6 x 10^5.

On a less technical note, computer related terms have slipped into more general conversation. Equality is something often used, both in mathematical and distinctly unmathematical situations. Obviously the *'='* sign is used to denote equality, but *'/='* (from the programming languages Ada and Fortran 90) or *'<>'* (from Pascal) are often used to denote inequality.

The tilde *'~'* is often used to indicate approximation. For example *'~50'* would mean *'approximately fifty'*.

The prefixing of words with an exclamation mark symbol, *'!'* is often used as a synonym for 'not' or 'no'. Thus, *'!idea'* means *'no idea'*.

HTML tags are used to indicate a particular mode of thought or type of concept. One of the most common 'net cliches' is the phrase '*<aol> me too! </aol>*'.

With reference to the service provider, America Online, whose users are held in some contempt by the rest of the Internet community, it illustrates that the user agrees with the previous point, but is aware that following up a post with 'me too!' is pathetic (and frequently referred to as such in netiquette documents).

Other uses for this device are the *<flame> ....</flame>* tags which indicate a flammable comment which isn't meant to be taken seriously.

Although a leading '>' has become the most popular inclusion convention, occasionally a *'#'* leader is used for quotations from authoritative sources. This alludes to the root prompt which starts with the hash symbol mentioned previously – a special Unix command prompt issued only to system administrators (it enables access to all the computer's systems).

Verb doubling

Supposed improvements to the English language, by these gallant pioneers of bits and bytes, are by all accounts logically definable into several different concepts.

One literary technique used frequently in more colloquial English is to double a verb in order to use it as an exclamation. 'Ding, Ding!' or 'Quack, Quack!' being good examples. Often meta-syntactic words (words which don't actually mean anything) are employed for this purpose online – *barf, foo, dang* and *bork* being some of the most common, as well as actions and events.

They are usually used at the end of a sentence, for impact. For example:

> *'Computers – you just love to hate them. Barf, barf!'*
>
> *'Do I look as if I care? Flame, flame!'*

Another culturism, which is somewhat related to this, are the Usenet 'joke' groups which have a tripled last element. The first such example being the newsgroup *alt.swedish.chef.bork.bork.bork,* but the passion quickly spread, leading to the infamous:

> *alt.wesley.crusher.die.die.die*
>
> *alt.pamela.anderson.sex.sex.sex*

and last, but certainly not least, *alt.billg.geek.geek.geek.* In fact the last one is a bit of a myth and it seems to have disappeared! Strange, but true – the Microsoft minions must be at work again!

Pluralisation

As well as pluralising words with the generally accepted 's', netizens have come up with some alternative alterations for this state of 'twoness, threeness, fourness'....you get the gist.

Yes, these innovative pioneers have made use of the little used 'z'. It is generally only applied to Internet related words, so hackers becomes hackerz, wares (pirated software) become warez and the list goes on. The pronunciation doesn't change, saving many tongue twisting moments trying to work out just how you're supposed to say it.

The use of the construction '-en' is common with words ending with the letter 'x'. So in the case of the case of the archaic MUD talker, VOX, the users of the system would not only be voxxers, but voxxen – in fact, the first term is generic, but the second tends to refer to female members.

Anthropomorphisation

Perhaps the most potentially disturbing aspect of online linguistic inventiveness is the tendency of technologists to assign human characteristics and feeling to clumps of cathode ray tubes and a couple of chips.

For example, it is not uncommon for one programmer to talk to another and say, 'it just collapsed under the strain' or worse 'the network switch box got confused'. It is certainly NOT uncommon to refer to a program dying, an action surely only applicable to animate objects.

What about me?

On a final note, just because a lot of people on the Net actually speak like this doesn't mean you have to. It's a common-held view that netizens use all this jargon and these buzz words to alienate users, but I have to say I don't think that is generally true.

In some cases jargon can make communication more important, but more importantly it lets users communicate not only ideas, but their feeling towards ideas, without actually stating it precisely – which is something we take for granted in the real world.

ASCII Art

If anything on the Net can be considered truly weird, I would imagine ASCII art just about tops the bill. It's probably most notorious in general Internet circles for taking its place in annoying 50 line signatures and flooding Usenet channels – the graffiti of Usenet, if you will.

Smileys are rather like the miniature form of a much bigger beast. The art form tends to reflect other aspects of popular Internet culture.

Beavis & Butthead – every nerd's friend

```
It's the classic story of two boys...sharing one brain....

            ,())))),
           ,()))))))),.        >>huh-huh<<          ,---,,,_
           ())))))))//((\     check it out,        (         ))  Plug into
          (\\( \))( \(/)    Beavis...we're,      (          )
          /(          \\  like, in "ASS-kee."   (          ) M T V
          //       _    \   >>huh-huh-huh<<     (_(_((((     )
          //   \  /    \   /                     (    , \    ) Music
          \   (.  .    \  /                      |   /   )   )
          (,     |     ,)    yeah. >>heh-heh<<   |\ /    (   ) Television
           \   ^\/^   /      that's COOL! hey,   (.(.)    S  )
           \          /     Butt-Head...you're    /_        \ )
            \ (-<>-) /          an "ASS-kee."  \  /__)   ^   \/
             \  --  /             >>heh-heh<<     /____/     |
              \ __ /                             )______     |
                |  |       //\/\\/\//\/\//\/\\\/\       \    |
             __-|__|-__    \                     /     __-\__|-__
            (          )   > BEAVIS AND BUTT-HEAD <    (          )
            |_|AC//DC|_|   /                     \    |_|METALL|_|
            | |      | |   \/\//\/\\/\\/\//\//\/\ TM  | |      | |  tif'94
```

Star Trek – to boldly go where no nerd has...

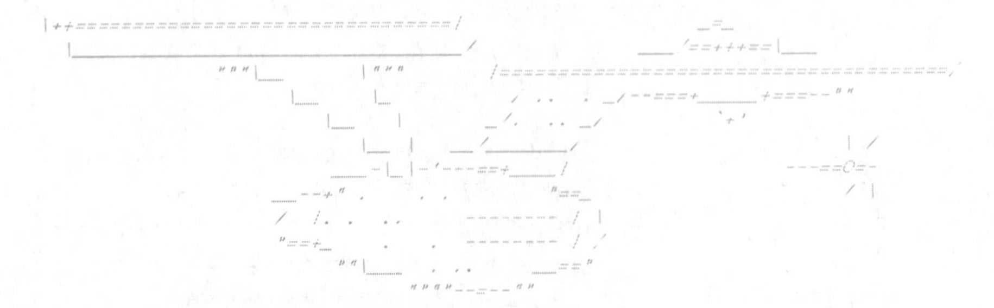

If you like this stuff, then firstly I recommend you see a doctor; secondly I would suggest you have a look at *http://www.chris.com/ascii_art_menu.html* which has a vast quantity of the stuff. Whatever your tastes – Dilbert to Ducks, Pammie to Presley, or even a trek through the stars – it's out there, somewhere!

Fixed character width

In order for the ASCII art to display properly you need to choose a font which uses a fixed character width. Courier, Monaco and FixedSys are usually pretty good bets.

ASCII art falls into two categories: line-ASCII and solid ASCII. Often the latter looks rather like an inversion of the former.

Making a start in ASCII art

The credit for this heading goes to Daniel Au, who has an art tutorial which is well worth reading at *http://www.geocities.com/SoHo/7373/dcau.htm.* If still suitably interested, a quick jolly to *http://www.geocities.com/SoHo/7373/faq.htm* is worthwhile as well. A few don'ts though...

DON'T post ASCII art to non ASCII Art groups on Usenet unless they fit into your four-line or less signature (for more about this, see Chapter Five).

DON'T remove people's signatures from their creations. Certainly DON'T steal them, and then call them your own.

DON'T mistake the Windows ANSI character set for ASCII, which incidentally is an ANSI character set as well, just smaller. If you do, many people won't be able to view your work.

DON'T insert HTML tags if people expect plain ASCII art. It may add some nice effects, but it looks lousy in a newsreader. Put a link to it on a web site, maybe.

On a final note

ASCII art may have a bit of a geeky image, but much of it is rather good. Just think, in 60 or 70 years time people may view this primitive art form in the same way many critics view Van Gogh, an artist not appreciated in his own time – then again, maybe not!

Words to Avoid

As well as there being a multitude of 'in' words to use on the Internet, there is also a (thankfully smaller) catalogue of 'not in' clangers for your literary delectation.

Clanger Identification

There are some words which, as soon as they leave your mouth, tell every net savvy person in the room that not only do you know nothing about the Internet but that (more dangerous still) you pretend you know something about it.

Indeed, there are a great many people who are just like that, but they do tend to fit into several distinct occupational groups so you can carefully avoid them in any social situation (nothing grates on a clued netizen's ears more).

Politicians just about top the list, but the sound of misinformation is music to all our ears. At least all those ears who listen to Newsnight. Al Gore, our American friend who is noted for getting the wrong end of the proverbial stick (together with Dan Quayle) did himself coin the phrase 'Information Superhighway' – which aptly proves my point.

Newspaper journalists get to No.2 on the hit parade, for their inability to articulate their thoughts about the Internet without resorting to corny cliches – personally I avoid them like the plague.

Finally come business executives who can't write a company report for shareholders without using the word 'cyberspace' or 'technological revolution' on every other page. I've managed to write a whole book on the darn thing without using either (this section excluded). Yeah, I'm just great aren't I?

Now that I've finished grinding my axe, if you fit into any of the above three groups, or now feel incredibly uneasy about expressing your vision of a future driven by technology, all I can say is 'welcome to the club'.

It's all a matter of perspective....

Aye, it is. If I followed Vint Cerf or Tim Berners-Lee onto a podium to give my view on the future of the Internet, I might well sound a right burk. Of course, the problem I've got isn't a lack of necessary vocabulary but a lack of credentials. The wannabe Net guru has two potential problems. Here I intend to help you with the first – bear in mind, however, you'll need to do something about the second.

'Information Superwotsit'

The reason why Information Superhighway is such a stupid word for the present day Internet is quite simple if you think about it. Firstly, they only have 'highways' in the States, whereas the Internet is a global beastie.

Secondly, in you go on a highway, road, whatever you want to call it, you are usually going somewhere. Conversely, on the Internet you can have enormous fun starting off somewhere, trying to get somewhere else, and then getting completely and utterly lost, whilst at the same time forgetting where you wanted to go in the first place.

Thirdly, and in light of the previous example, quite fortunately real highways have signposts, whilst the Internet has hardly any, and most of those point in opposite directions.

In 'The Road Ahead' Bill Gates talks about the future of the Internet as being the Information Superhighway. This may indeed be accurate. Let not a mere mortal such as myself, question the visions of a god – but, here and now, there is no Infobahn, no *via datum,* no motorway, road, bridleway or footpath of technological persuasion, whatsoever.

'Cyberspace'

This was a term coined by William Gibson's novel, 'Neuromancer,' written in 1982. His near-total ignorance of computers enabled him to speculate about the role of computers and hacker culture in the future in ways that Internet users have since found extremely naive, but rather thrilling at the same time.

The idea of a 'Tron-like' Internet seems as futuristic today as the film of the same name looks dated.

Of course, 'cyberspace' doesn't just come unstuck due to overly optimistic, technically rosy and wildly inaccurate observations (or lack thereof) – the etymology of the word differs rather from its modern day application. That in itself is nothing new, but then it's only a twenty year old word!

The term 'cyber' actually comes from the Greek *'kubernetes'* which means 'to steer or govern'. It entered English from the French to form the word *'cybernetics'* – the theory of control and communication processes. This eventually came to be associated with automated control and everything and anything robotic.

'So what,' I hear you cry 'this isn't a history lesson.' True, true. Unfortunately the modern connotations of the word are no more an accurate definition of a living, breathing, enhanced interactive Internet than those of our Greek and French friends.

As the Internet becomes more and more accessible, which certainly is one aspect of a visionary cyberspace, the technology in comparison becomes less and less important. Of course, it wouldn't all hang together without it, but people don't logon to the modern Internet to fiddle with, or worse, talk to computers – rather they nitter natter away to other people.

The result is that the people who use the Internet are just as important as the technology that makes it all work, and to most people certainly more interesting. Surely better to call it a network of people, than a network of automatons? William Gibson obviously thought not.

Not just what you say, but the way you say it

Speaking or writing about the Internet can be much more perilous than these last few pages perhaps indicate. Sometimes it only takes really small things to alert every egghead in the room to the fact you are a little technologically inept. In the same way that interior designers cringe at DIY programmes, car salesmen cringe at 'TV motor experts' and French people cringe at English people trying to speak French (okay, perhaps not in quite the same way!) it is true that a little syllable out here, a possessive wrong there, make Internet diehards sit on their hands, clammer to get out of the room, or unfortunately and more commonly, stand up and tell you what a twit you are.

It's 'the' Internet

One bleeper that newbies often make is to talk about *'Internet'. 'Internet is a great thing, you can do so many cool things on Net'* as they talk amongst themselves, as one person stifles a snigger whilst everyone else nods in vague agreement. Remember, there are many networks, indeed many 'i'nternets, but there is only one Internet with a capital 'I'.

Synonyms

Just as the English have a quite superfluous number of words for the great toilet, the digerati have a ridiculous number of names for this new fangled thing.

Younger people, with their tendency to shorten words, call it 'the Net'. People who don't know anything about it, but pretend to be experts call it 'the Super Highway' or suchlike. This book tends to use lots of different words to describe it, to make for a good and varied reading experience. Conversely, technical people tend to stick to one word, the most accurate definition – 'the Internet'.

People who like to be cool and hip call it 'cyberspace' and people who want to be prophetic call it the 'technological revolution' – the list goes on...

Computers, PCs, machines, microcomputers – the Internet isn't the only synonym-crazy literary object of moment. The moral of the story is, however, use the right words and even if YOU don't know what you're talking about, people will think you do!

Smileys and Emoticons

Emoticons allow users who want to communicate the tone as well as the content of the message, but feel quite incapable of doing this efficiently through the use of standard literary techniques. A brief list of the most common emoticons is shown below:

Smileys

Many of these are used by people not because they want to convey a meaning specific to the smiley, but they just happen to like the look of that particular one:

:-)	Smiling	;-)	Winking
:-D	Laughing	:->	Cackling
;-P	Ironic	:’’’-)	Crying
:-(	Unhappy	%-)	Drunk
$-)	Greedy	:-*	Kissing

And for the romantics among us...

@--``-,--``-,,--   Rose

Emoticons

Most other emoticons (ie, those contained with asterisks or angle brackets) are fairly self explanatory.

grin   <hugs>   *smile*   <laff>   *chuckle*

If someone says *‘ROTFL’* after a joke, that means ‘Rolling on the floor laughing’. *‘ROTFLMAO’* has the same gist – it’s just slightly less polite....

In IRC you can also use the ‘/me’ to suggest actions. For example, if I typed *‘/me falls off his chair and laffs hysterically’* (in case you hadn’t noticed ‘laff’ is another ‘kewl’ mispelling – apparently anyway!) then that would come up in the channel as *‘* Joshy falls off his chair and laffs hysterically’*. Make sure you write it in the third person, else it will sound rather strange.

Defining the Cyber Patois

There are many different buzz words which have winnowed their way across the Internet. This short glossary contains the most common through to the most unusual of Internet jargon. Without further ado . . .

AFAIK – As Far As I Know.

AFK – Away From Keyboard.

AOL – America Online is one of the world's largest service providers, allowing not only connection to the Internet, but to their own online services.

ASCII – American Standard Code for Information Interchange. A plain text format which is universally readable.

asl? or *a/s/l?* – They are asking you to state your Age, Sex and Location.

Attachment – A file or binary which is included with e-mails.

Bandwidth – A measure of the maximum amount of data that at any one time can be transmitted from one machine to another.

Barf – A term of disgust, or a mistake.

BBIAB – Be Back In A Bit.

BBL – Be Back Later.

BBS – Bulletin Board System. A computer system, which may or may not have a full connection to the Internet, where members can dial in, leave messages, play games, send e-mail, but more commonly download pornography. A dying breed.

Bf – Boyfriend.

BFN – Bye For Now.

Binaries – A generic term for files which are not intelligible in plain text form (ie, although HTML may not be plain text, you can read it in plain text form). These are most commonly pictures and programs.

BOFH – ******* Operator From Hell. A particularly unpleasant network administrator.

Bounced Mail – Electronic Mail which has been returned to its sender, usually because the destination address is invalid.

BRB – Be Right Back.

BTW – By The Way.

CDA – Communications Decency Act. Part of the American Senate's telecommunications reforms of 1996.

CFV – Call For Votes. Before a ballot is held on Usenet at the end of a discussion, typically on a newsgroup creation request, a CFV is sent to all the relevant groups.

Chop – Channel operator, with reference to IRC.

Client – A program that accesses information across a network, or exchanges data with a server of some sort. Web browsers, newsreaders and e-mail programs can be generically referred to as 'clients'.

Cracker – A criminal hacker (see *hacker)*.

Clue or *Cloo* – A term attributed to net savvy individuals.

Cya – See you (later).

C$ – A rather derogatory abbreviation for CompuServe, with reference to their steep time charges.

Daemon – A UNIX background operation. Usually such programs are identified by a 'd' at the end of their name. The IRC server program is a daemon, hence 'ircd'.

DCC – Direct Client to Client. Used in IRC to conduct direct conversations and exchange of binary data.

Domain – A hostname which is used to identify its users to the network *(eg,* my domain is *journalism.demon.co.uk).*

Download – Transfer of a file from one computer system to another.

E-Mail – Electronic Mail is a correspondence system which allows you to transmit text, pictures, sounds and other digitized material across the world in a matter of seconds. See Chapters One and Five.

E-zine – An electronic magazine, usually in the form of an interactive web page.

FAQ – Frequently Asked Questions. See Chapter Seven.

Finger – A utility usually used to supply information about the owner of an e-mail address.

Firewall – A security system used to restrict and control traffic travelling from an insecure network to a secure network.

Fidonet – An old BBS style computer network, popular in the UK.

Flame – An abusive attack upon someone online.

FOAD – **** Off And Die (in its most polite permutation at least).

Freeware – Programmes which are distributed on a non-profit basis. They can often be 'open source' as well, which enables the source code to be updated and transferred between platforms easily.

FTP – File Transfer Protocol. The standard method of transferring files over the Internet.

FUBAR – ****** Up Beyond All Recognition.

FWIW – For What It's Worth.

FYI – For Your Information.

Gf – Girlfriend.

GIF – Graphic Image File Format. Brought to fame by CompuServe, it employs LZW compression and is very common on the Web.

Gopher – A menu based system for retrieving Internet archives, usually archived by subject. Generally superseded by the WWW.

GTG – Got To Go.

Hacker – A technically savvy computer enthusiast who derives joy from exploring other people's computer systems, although not necessarily with any intent to damage.

Handle – A name by which someone is identified on a MUD.

Hehe – Written representation of laughter. Non-English speakers also say *'jeje'*.

HTH – Hope This Helps (often bitterly ironic).

HTML – HyperText Markup Language. A scripting language with which web pages are constructed.

IIRC – If I Recall Correctly.

IM(H)O – In My (Humble) Opinion.

IME – In My Experience.

(the) Internet – A global decentralised network comprised of many other networks and systems which enables the instantaneous exchange of large amounts of data.

IOW – In Other Words.

IP – Internet Protocol. It defines the system by which packets of information travel between nodes.

IRC – Internet Relay Chat. See Chapters One and Four.

ISP – Internet Service Provider. The people who provide your gateway to the Internet.

IWBNI – It Would Be Nice If . . .

IYSWIM – If You See What I Mean . . .

J/K – Just Kidding.

JPEG – Joint Photographic Experts Group. A compressed graphics format used frequently on the Web.

Kill file – A newsreader file in which you can enter keywords, e-mail addresses and user names to stop yourself having to read unwanted Usenet articles.

KOTC – Kiss On The Cheek.

LOL – Laughing Out Loud.

LTNS – Long Time, No See.

L8R – (See you) Later.

Microsoft – The world's most successful software business, the company we all love to hate. The CEO is Bill Gates, boy wonder of the 1980s, industry giant of the 90s.

MIME – Multipurpose Internet Mail Extensions. A standard for the transfer of binary e-mail attachments.

Mirror – An identical FTP or WWW site set up to reduce the strain and share the traffic directed towards a particular site.

MMF – Make Money Fast. A genre of unsolicited commercial e-mail and Usenet spam.

Modem – Modulator/Demodulator. A device that converts digital signals produced by the computer to analog signals suitable for transmission over the traditional telephone.

MSG – Message.

Multi-task – When a computer is capable of performing more than one operation at the same time.

MUD – Multi-User Dungeons, also *MIST, MUSH, MUCK,* etc.

Netiquette – Network Etiquette, a cultural code of conduct; a dignified, but not universally agreed, standard of behaviour expected on the Internet.

Netscape – Microsoft's main opponent in the web browser wars, producers of Netscape Navigator and the Netscape Communicator Suite.

Newbie – A newcomer to the Net, or one particular area of it.

Newsgroup – Usenet message forum, organised by subject hierarchy.

NNTP – Network News Transfer Protocol, the gubbins behind the transfer of Usenet articles, from server to server and from server to client.

Node – Any device that is individually identifiable to a network.

OTOH – On The Other Hand.

OSPs – Online Service Providers. They provide their own content in addition to Internet connectivity (eg, CompuServe, AOL and BT Lineone).

Packet – A unit of data, which is transferred across the network using TCP/IP, and includes information about where it is from, where it is going, and data checksums (which make sure the data arrives in the same condition it leaves), in addition to the main body of data itself.

Packet Loss – The failure to transmit data from one host to another, which can result in data exchange taking a very long time (eg, packet loss of 50% would double the time taken for data transfer).

Phreaker – Someone who hacks telephone systems.

Ping – A program that sends a small packet of time-stamped data that measures how far away, in electronic terms at least, one host is from another host.

POP3 – Post Office Protocol 3. An e-mail protocol that lets you pick up your mail, even if you connect through someone else's account.

Protocol – An agreed standard for network devices to exchange information with each other.

POV – Point Of View.

PPL – People.

Re: – With reference to:

Re – IRC term short for *rehi:* saying hello to a channel or person for a second or subsequent time.

RFC – Request For Comment. Internet documents that are gospel on 'mutually' agreed standards.

RL – Real Life.

ROFL – Rolling On The Floor, Laughing.

RTFM – Read The Flipping Manual. Often in response to a question answered in an FAQ.

Server – A machine which primarily exchanges data with other servers and offers data to hosts.

SMTP – Simple Mail Trasfer Protocol. A method of transporting electronic mail across the cyber ether.

Spam – A Usenet article that is inappropriately posted to numerous, often irrelevant, groups.

Streaming – Files which are delivered and viewed (or heard) in 'real-time' rather than waiting for the whole file to download before being run.

TCP/IP – Transmission Control Protocol/Internet Protocol. A protocol suite which is the mechanical dooda behind the Internet today. It enables the exchange of information between nodes.

Telnet – An Internet protocol that allows you to log on to a remote computer as a terminal, to use its resources remotely.

TTBOMK – To The Best Of My Knowledge.

TTFN – Ta Ta, For Now.

Unix – A rather elegant operating system, which most people really don't want to see (the lack of pretty pictures perturbs them), but is a common favourite for Microsoft haters, academics and Internet propeller heads.

URL – Uniform Resource Locator. The addressing system used to identify sites to web browsers (eg, *http://www.journalism.demon.co.uk*) would be a URL. Microsoft likes to call them Internet shortcuts.

Usenet – Users' Network. See Chapters One and Five.

UUnencode – A method of converting binary files into text so they can be attached to e-mails or Usenet posts. Rather like MIME, but older.

Warez – Pirated software (pronounced 'wares').

Wb – Welcome back.

Wizard – An 'immortal' MUD character.

WTF – What The ****?

WWW – World Wide Web.

WYSIWYG – What You See Is What You Get.

YMMV – Your Mileage May Vary.

'Zipped up' – A file which has been compressed using the ever popular 'Pkzip'.

Chapter Four

Instantaneous Communication Media

In this chapter we discuss the pros, cons and effects of real time communications on the Internet as well as who uses them and why.

Covers

What is 'Real Time'?

Internet resources, facilities and services can be divided into two groups: those which are interactive, and those which are passive.

A web page, for example, is mainly passive – although it may have an e-mail address or a bulletin board to which you can supply comment, it is primarily a one way medium.

Conversely, IRC, Usenet, MUDs and E-Mail are all examples of interactive media in that they accept input from two or more parties.

These interactive services can further be divided into those which offer 'real time' communication and those which offer 'delayed response' communication. Of the services mentioned previously, IRC and MUDs fall into the former category, whilst Usenet and e-Mail fall into the latter. This is, however, by no means an exhaustive list!

The advantages of 'real time' communication are many. Michael Lawrie, a man once styled as the Information Super Highwayman, and the driving force behind the split of IRCNet from EfNet, thought that the only way to have a debate was in real time, since anyone could put together a reasonable argument if they had several hours to do it. Essentially, discussion in real time requires more skill than in delayed response forums.

Despite this, or indeed for exactly those reasons, there is little serious debate on IRC. Games in particular are much more exciting in a real time environment and you can learn much more about a person in an hour on IRC than you perhaps would on Usenet. If you so desire.

This is an important point. On IRC you have much more control over the direction of a conversation, since information is usually gained in response to direct questions. On Usenet the stimuli on which a response is based is not usually a question, but rather another person's answer.

Effects of Remoteness

It is very easy to forget, when using the Internet, that the people on the other end of the line are human.

This is a result of the psychological mind-set that computer users adopt: that what you type into a computer doesn't matter, because the computer doesn't have feelings or opinions. Most operators have their own PC and no-one else really uses it.

Just because you can't see, touch or hear someone on the Net, it doesn't mean they aren't there.

This concept of free expression, which is often suppressed to prevent social incidents in real life, is lavishly employed online.

Without leaping onto a bandwagon of sophistry, just because you can't see, touch or hear someone on the Net, it doesn't mean they aren't there.

Particularly with open forums such as newsgroups you never know who is reading it – indeed, these Usenet lurkers could be your boss, your bank manager or your best friend.

Bearing this in mind, you should never say anything on the Internet that you wouldn't say in real life, or at least nothing that you would not jump up and say in a room full of ten, a hundred or a thousand people.

Let us not stretch this out of proportion, however. The chances of you actually being unlucky enough to say the wrong thing to the wrong person are slim, especially when you consider there are over 3 million Internet users in the UK alone.

Flaming

The finely honed art of flaming gets a big section all of its own in Chapter Five, but this craft is practised by some people who, if you were to meet them in real life, would seem really rather tame. Being remote in a physical sense from other people makes users think that they can project a different, more foreboding personality on other netizens in just the same way as they can project a more impressive physical description of themselves. They can't.

'Lag' and 'Netsplits'

These two little beasties are the bane of real time communication. IRC networks operate in the same decentralised way as the Internet itself, but there are usually two or three servers (with quick connections) which form the backbone of the network. These are called 'hub' servers whilst the servers which are connected to them are called 'leaf' servers.

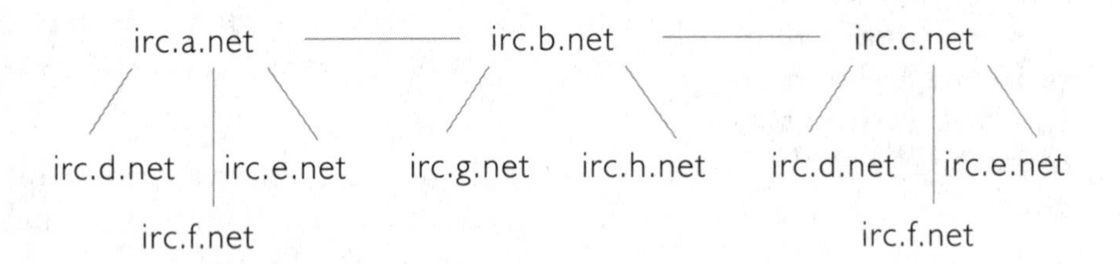

On some servers, you can bring up a list of its C/N lines by typing '/stats c' or '/stats n' respectively in the 'status' or 'command' window. You can also get a diagrammatic view of the network by typing '/links'.

IRC Network basics

IRC network links work on the basis of C/N lines. A 'C' line instructs a server to update another server, whilst an 'N' line instructs a server to receive data from another server. Therefore, every 'C' line must have an 'N' line at the other end.

Now, the subject of how to route servers can be quite interesting, but it is rather beyond the scope of this book. However, the effect it has on users is not, so we'll delve a little further.

When things go wrong

Sometimes the links between the servers break. Where this break occurs will decide its overall effect on the network. For example, if there was an outage (things break) between irc.a.net and irc.b.net then the left hand server group would be separated from the rest of the network and you would no longer be able to talk to anyone on the irc.b.net or irc.c.net rings and *vice versa*. This is called a netsplit.

Lag

'Lag' is a quite different phenomenon. Electronically speaking the time taken to transmit information from one node to another node is known as your 'lag'. It is measured using a facility called 'ping' which sends off a small data packet to a recipient, which the recipient replies to.

Lag and IRC

With IRC, if your ping time is less than 10 seconds (or less than 20 in a channel) the speed of transmission is usually sufficient to hold a reasonable conversation.

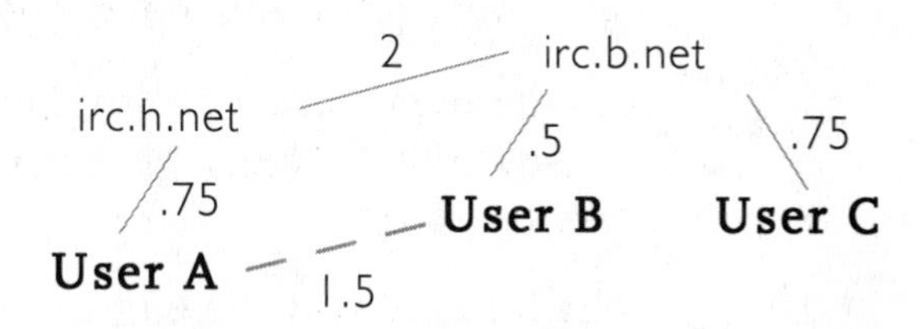

Your 'lag' to different people will vary. In the network section above, if User B wanted to talk to User C across the network (on IRC this would take place via a private message box or a channel) then it would take approximately 1.25 seconds for User C to receive the data and 1.25 seconds for User B to receive the reply. In addition to the time taken to write the messages, and processing time (which is usually negligible) there would be a lag of 3 seconds between the two users. That is fairly good.

Across the network, User A is (0.75+2+0.5=) 3.25 seconds distant from User B, so it would take one of the users at least 7 seconds to receive a response after inputting a question.

In the next section, we talk about the difference between DCC Chats and private message boxes. If User B and User A were to hold a DCC Chat the response time would be 3 seconds (1.5 seconds for a single trip), which is much better than the 7 seconds you would get from a private message (across the network) and much less likely to break since the route taken is more direct.

Connection theory is pretty complicated, but putting it into practice exacerbates the problem, because 'lag' is a dynamic variable and changes with the amount of traffic passing across the pipes. Suffice to say that weird things can happen with replies being received (by third parties) before queries and users mysteriously disappearing. Fascinating or not, if you don't understand why something is happening, it's probably something to do with this.

Lag and Games

This is a whole different kettle of fish, but it is a bit simpler as there is only *one* server and, essentially for a user, only *one* connection to worry about.

The demands are a bit tougher. In most action games such as Doom or Netrek a ping over one second, can be well, ermm....fatal.

The options vary depending on the game, although the easiest solution involves changing servers to another which is electronically closer to you. You can also alter the 'packet send' or 'update request' rates which can have a marginal effect, or turn off error checking.

Signal error is another problem which does tend to loom over laggy connections, but not exclusively so. It can cause bad connections since any bits which are 'in error' have to be re-sent.

One-to-one Communication

In a similar way to real life, a lot of the people you will talk to on IRC or any other real time communications medium you will find incredibly boring. Indeed, after the initial pleasantries you may not want to ask them anything at all. There are a few fairly typical things that are often said when you start up a private conversation with somebody.

'a/s/l . . . .?'

After the almost universally recognised 'hello' in its various permutations (hi/'ello/lo/re/howdy....) you wait a few seconds while it is revealed whether this person actually wants to speak to you, during which time you hope they reciprocate the acknowledgement, like it is some kind of required morse code signal. It's there because it's deemed impolite to burst right into the background establishment stage, but then again courtesy isn't always one of IRC's strong points, and nor is standardisation – which is rather fortunate, else it would be an awfully boring place.

You could spend several minutes trying to work out exactly what *'asl?'* means. I certainly did, but since the point of this book is to turn you into an enlightened addition to the Internet ilk, it is an abbreviation asking for your *'a'*ge, your *'s'*ex and your *'l'*ocation. The usual response format is something along the lines of *19/m/oxford.* If you want to be really flash you can get your IRC client to pop that up when you press a button, which will save you typing it in. (Except that would be really sad and nerdy, and of course, we don't do sad and nerdy! I'm a trendy 'cyberspace' writer now, if I did things like that they might actually think I knew something about the wretched thing. Ha, what a novel idea!)

Making a good impression

Initial impressions are important. I probably get a private 'msg' (message) or 'dcc chat' (same kind of thing) about every ten minutes. About 75% of the people who 'msg' me online are people I've never spoken to before, and of this 75%, I respond to about half.

Only about two-thirds of this 37% actually arouse my interest sufficiently that I can bear talking to them for more than 5 minutes, and even then there are only about 6% left who I'll ever type a digital utterance to again.

Result? I have spent close to a thousand hours online in the last few years and there have only been about four or five people who I've talked to regularly over a 6-month period. Maybe twice that number fairly represents those people who I'd probably quite like to talk to, but never see around any more.

Conclusion? Most people on the Internet are boring as hell, but if you stick at it long enough it can be quite rewarding.

Are you 'interesting' or 'boring'?

This is a question you probably can't answer. The strange thing about the Internet is that you may have the social skills of a newt in real life and be the life and soul of the digital party online, but generally speaking there are some social skills which correlate between both areas.

In real life it isn't always so important, particularly in large social circles or at work. Indeed, if you think of how many people you have deep, meaningful or really interesting conversations with in one month, my proposed (and, incidentally, entirely contrived) statistics don't seem quite so weird.

The main difference is that communication on the Infobahn is generally much more information intensive than it is in real life. Now, the problem lies in that you can't do just that (lie that is), because frankly lots of people won't believe you have starred in four Hollywood blockbusters. Shame.

This intensity can make things a bit topsy turvy. Take the saddest, most boring bloke who works in your office: the one who is really rather nice and brings you coffee every morning, but wears the wrong coloured socks and makes peculiar grunting and squealing noises while reading the Garfield cartoons in the paper.

Now, think of that stunning girl who works on the ground floor of your office, or that hunk who has walked straight off the cover of a teenage-girl's magazine and onto your shop-floor. You think: 'That is someone I would really like to get to know!' Hey, am I psychic or what?

The strange thing is that the sad nerdy type with all his quirks and peculiarities has probably a lot more to talk about than someone who sends hormones fizzing around your body. Why?

Well more than likely it's because he's the one who sits up at night thinking about what he ought to say, or what he ought to do to make himself more interesting or exciting. The same perhaps could not be said for someone born beautiful, or someone hugely successful, and therefore accustomed to the constant attentions of others.

On the Internet it is useful to have a strong personality and the ability to communicate and amplify your persona.

Writing skill is an advantage. You often get quite a few boring technical types who are very intelligent in their way and have quirks in abundance, but can't write interestingly.

Despite all this, you shouldn't drag out this stereotyping too far. The kind of person that *you* will enjoy whiling away summer nights talking to will obviously depend on your individual criteria. The need to be 'different' on the Internet is important, but the need to be yourself is even greater.

Chat or Msg?

Knowing the difference between these two forms of communication is useful. A message, which is initiated using the '/msg' function, operates by taking a message from user A, sending it to user A's server, and passing it along to user B's server which then gives it to user B.

In this sense it actually utilises the IRC network to transmit the communique, which ultimately makes it rather slow as it takes a very 'round-about' route to its destination.

Unlike messaging, DCC Chat is a Direct-Client-to-Client system, but isn't really anything to do with IRC at all. Although it is featured in most modern clients, you must be aware that for those using UNIX variants or Telnet, dealing with DCC chats can be awfully difficult.

Sometimes the servers will split, splitting all private messages between the servers, but with a DCC Chat session the communication should still be maintained, assuming that the same network break which caused the netsplit doesn't block the route between the two users.

Often, when you approach someone for the first time it is preferable to do so through a private message rather than a DCC. Quite simply, the recipient doesn't have to 'accept' a private message (although you can block a user, by utilising the /ignore command) so you will be able to stun your potential conquest with your flowing prose and engage their interest, without them having to lift a finger.

Finding the Talkers

Channels (or technically speaking, channels which support 'modes') are prefixed by a hash (#) sign.

Finding people who are likely respondents and likely to have similar interests to you is difficult. One way to find people with defined characteristics is to look through channels.

If you want to go in for some intellectually highbrow discussion then messaging someone from #atheism might seem a good idea. If football is more your thing then looking down the user list for #soccer is an equally feasible proposition.

Some channels can be misleading, particularly with geographical locations. #england, for example, is filled out with Anglo-American wannabes, and English expatriates as well as UK residents.

A good method of finding users who fit into a specific profile is to use the '/who' command. Now, one disadvantage of this is that many clients set their users '+i', which means they don't turn up in 'who' lists (which spam bots, used to advertise web sites).

Domains

IRC commands are prefixed with a 'slash' (/) – eg, /who, /me.

Despite this, by entering a command such as '/who *uk' you will get a fairly extensive list of UK based users. The 'star' or asterisk is known as a 'wildcard' which is a short way of saying 'list everything that ends with 'uk''. You could also use egg*, which would list everything that began with egg, so eggy.co.uk, eggs.clara.net and eggaps.u-net.com would all show up. Alternatively, you could try *twinky* which would list everything with the complete string 'twinky' anywhere within it. This search is conducted based on the users' domains.

A domain can be expressed in several different ways. The most basic is called a 'numeric dotted quad'. IP addresses as they are generically known are issued by ISPs in various quantities, although due to the huge expansion of the Internet, they are fast becoming a precious resource.

For example, Demon Internet, who are based in the UK and Netherlands, were one of the first commercial ISPs, so they were allocated a substantial number of different addresses. As a result, each of their customers get their own IP address, and no-one else uses it when they aren't logged on.

DNS stands for Domain Name System. What it essentially does is take a numeric IP address and tag a text name to it.

Take for example my IP address, *'193.237.88.202'*. This numeric address is stored on Demon's DNS server. What this DNS does, amongst other things, is let a rather long winded string of numbers be identified as a more memorable text value – in my case *'journalism.demon.co .uk'*.

These numeric addresses are issued in blocks, which come in three different types. A class C block would give an Internet node 256 addresses (*'193.237.88.*'*) – the 'wildcard' once again tells us that anything could be included in the last section. The last string of numbers ranges from 0 to 255, hence the size of the issue.

A Class B block lets you specify all the numbers in the last *two* sections. The possible combinations allow you to have tens of thousands of addresses. Finally, a Class A block only specifies the first block, which gives you loads and loads of addresses you can issue, but these large allocations are rather prized and only the largest of organisations get given them.

On a culture related note, you'll hear a lot of users complaining that they don't get static IPs – they have to share, effectively. Many newer service providers aren't issued sufficient numbers to give one to each of their customers so they simply assign a different number to each modem. Obviously, a user doesn't 'dial into' the same modem each time so their IP address changes each time they log on.

The problems with dynamic IPs are apparent when you want to find users. Particularly on networks which don't offer you the ability to register and reserve names, it can be hard to identify users who don't have a recognisable address. Put simply, I would be easy to find, even if I wasn't using my regular nickname, because if you did a '/who' on **journalism.demon.co.uk*, only my name would turn up. Users who don't get issued static IPs get meaningless addresses like *du-15.clara.net* (modem no. 15) so you can't identify who that user is.

One of the few advantages with dynamic IPs is that they do offer a certain degree of anonymity. If you look at my address and bung a *'www'* in front of it in a web browser, you would be able to find my web page. Of course you don't have to put up a web page, but if you do, don't be surprised if some users seem to know you rather well, yet you've never ever spoken to them before. Clever stuff eh?

'For he looked upon his domain and wept'

Using the '/who' command might not help you find Alexander the Great, at least not without a bit of temporal flux, but in some ways it can be rather nifty. If, for example, you typed '/who *ox.ac.uk' you would get a list of all the people who are logged in through Oxford University's Internet porthole.

Now even if talking to ubiquitous undergrads isn't your thing, you can use a table of domains to help pinpoint interesting bods who you might want to talk to, but more importantly, who might want to talk to you. Don't make your search too vague though, else you'll get a huge message kludge and spend half an hour trying to read through the results.

Element	*Description*	*Geography*	*Examples*
ac	Academic (16+)	Country specific (not US)	ox.ac.uk, hdk.ac.pl
com	Commercial (ISP user)	International	computerstep.com
co	Commercial (ISP user)	Country specific	tesco.co.uk
edu	Education	Mostly US / Not specific	indiana.edu, mit.edu
gov	Government related	International, but can be specific	www.gov.uk, www.us.gov
net	Network resource (traditionally)	International, but can be specific	smtp.demon.net, clara.net
org	Not-for-profit organisation	International, but can be specific	labour.org.uk, ml.org

Code	*Country*
au	Australia
br	Brazil
ca	Canada
dl	Germany
fr	France
jp	Japan
uk	United Kingdom
us	US (eg, wa.us, ny.us)

These tables list various ISO 'type' codes and elements of domains which are extremely useful in identifying people.

Control and issue

Domains which relate to the UK – ie, *org.uk* or *ac.uk* or *co.uk* amongst others – are issued by Nominet.

International domains such as *.com* or *.net* are issued by Internic, who are based in Virginia, US.

Every domain needs to be linked to an IP address. The IP addresses (the numbers) are issued by RIPE, which just complicates things further.

Group Communication

Talking in a group, as any socially aware person probably realises, is very different from talking to one other person.

Some people feel more comfortable and prefer the former situation; others prefer the intensity of a personal conversation.

Intensity

Getting to know people on the Internet, being the deep and meaningful experience that it is, is rather like playing a guitar. It's much better to play a few songs well than a whole repertoire of songs badly. Therefore, it's better to know a few people really well than know lots of people as vague recollections.

Conversely, the advantage of groups or channels is that they don't demand participation, other than a 'hello' when you a join, a 'bye' when you leave and a few cyber-giggles interspersed therein.

This allows you the luxury of lurking and just reading, which is a much less exhausting activity than actually having to tip-tap away on your keyboard. There is nothing more annoying than trying to talk to someone in a private chat when they take five minutes to respond to a question. If lethargy is your thing, don't even think about trying to embroil yourself with conversation you can't handle.

Multi-channelling

REMEMBER

Multi-channelling is when you sit in several different channels at once.

Rather than another offspring from the pig pen of hi-fi featurism, multi-channelling is a fine art. Lurking in several channels at once is a good way to get to know new people and find out what kind of environment you feel most at home in – relaxed, intellectual, gossipy or, heaven forbid, even prudish. Many channels operate a system by which lurkers are kicked out after spending a certain amount of time idling and not saying anything. It is considered polite not to join more channels than you can possibly read, unless you are a 'regular'.

What you do is you 'listen in' on a few channels and find people who you think you might find interesting and then talk to them privately. This approach has the advantage that they already 'know' you, on a superficial psychological level at least, because they've seen you in the channel list.

Geography and the 'lurk factor'

Intermittent channel participation and idleness is much more common from users across the pond, because over in that enlightened land they don't have annoying regulatory bodies who make them pay for local, cheap rate calls.

The result is rather interesting. Along with the periodic hoo-haa over how the Internet is going to die, due to insufficient infrastructure, came the argument that free calls encouraged the squandering of bandwidth.

American users often spend a great deal of time online, doing very little, so the extra network load isn't very profound, but what you do find is a lot of dumb Americans.

Dumb in the sense of not speaking; and neither do they listen. For the sake of harmonious international relations, 'inactive' might be a better word, but whatever you want to call it, if you try and talk to a yank at 11am, he's probably still curled up in bed.

Cogito ergo sum. I think therefore I am, but a nation state is an exception to every philosophical rule – just because you can see them (in the channel list), it doesn't mean they are there!

Channels for 'boring' people

One undeniable fact about IRC is that people with similar interests tend to congregate in certain channels. It may take you days, months even to find a channel you really feel at home in, but it is worth it! Everyone has their Martini club, the kind of place which they find communicatively beautiful.

The problem is that the hardened mixers and shakers of the intoxicating cyber-drink can be fine connoisseurs of the weird, the wacky and the funny. Those with these qualities of Internet individuality, textual tenacity and, of course, similar interests tend to clump together in little groups. So they are difficult to find individually.

With one-to-one communication you really get to find out what people are like, where as the background noise produced by 'channel babble' can set all the people who you want to find awash and drowning in a sea of boring nitter natter. Intrinsically, channels aren't so bad at finding people who you really want to talk to, but they are bloomin' rubbish for actually conducting a conversation at length.

A tangled web we weave

Aside from a short, digressive demonstration of the appalling quality of puns in technology writing (science and illiteracy, huh?), when you consider that a fair number of people in a channel are talking to other people in a channel, and even then some of them may be talking to the same people in other channels, it can get all very weird.

This makes IRC the absolute epitome of a gossip breeding medium. You may only exchange words with a person a few times, but you might know quite a bit about them, and the opposite may be true as well. Opinions are formed and more rarely broken on the basis of what other people think.

The general trend of channel evolution is that things become factionalised, and things get a bit 'groupie', with users making generalisations about other people based on who they are believed to talk to.

A rather clever process, since it is often what happens behind the scenes which determines who visits where, rather than actually what happens in the channel itself.

This volatility and the issue of online cliques makes IRC a very different place from the one which is most commonly envisaged. So beware, and remember that gossip should never be taken at face value: judge people for yourself.

Turning off

If all else fails, never forget that you can just turn everything off. Everyone makes social blunders online, and often you don't feel any better about them than if you had made them in real life.

Sometimes getting out into the real world and unplugging the phone extension for a few days can help clear the mind, get your moral objectiveness back in place and help you deal with the problem.

Don't get into the habit of thinking *'well it's alright if I upset people – it's not real'.* Just because it is unlike communication in any conventional sense, it doesn't mean it isn't real. You should apply the same standards to what you type into your keyboard as what you would say in real life. You should treat people with the same respect as you would in real life. Strangely most people don't have any problem conducting themselves appropriately in a room full of people, yet many seem unable to show courtesy in an IRC channel.

Because the Internet has a limited impact on the rest of your life, it enables you to do things which you wouldn't normally do. This is often abused, however wading through the cyber-ether can be your opportunity to be truthful, helpful and gregarious, and everything else you don't have the time or the ability to be in real life.

IRC Cliques and Politics

IRC cliques are much less obvious than in delayed response media like Usenet. There are two main reasons for this. Firstly, it isn't generally a confrontational environment, so there is rarely an opportunity to take sides and when this does happen, the immediacy of response stops the participants from forgetting that there is a human 'at the end of the line'.

Secondly, IRC is a naturally 'groupie' forum with people divided up into different channels, with a vast, almost limitless opportunity for overlap. Channels are apparent as separate entities in themselves and easy to create, so users don't have to co-exist in a group with those they would rather not chat to.

However, cliques and 'playground' politics do exist.

Policy

The usual cause for division is over channel policy. If you think of politics in real life as venal and vicious, then online channel politics are all that and pointless as well.

Users who are similar in both attitudes and interests will tend to 'stick together' and talk to each other. Trying to reconcile the 'carefree' lobby with the 'rule and regulation' group will only result in tears and anguish.

Most people eventually learn to 'Do The Right Thing™', but I speak from the experience of trying to 'win over' other IRC users to my (enlightened) belief in anti-control – it just isn't worth the effort.

REMEMBER

Channel Operators are the people who control individual channels.

The real problem is that netizens who start channels, and to a much greater extent, 'admins' who set up servers, tend to be the most rabid of control freaks, with their desire for control being proportional to the time they are willing to invest setting things up.

'Services networks' (ie, networks that allow channel registration) are the worst channels of all for pathetic rules and picky regulations. On a network such as Dalnet, the founder of the channel doesn't have to have the support of his 'chops' (channel operators) in order to set his rules, whereas on an unregulated network like EfNet, there maybe a nominal 'founder', but he relies upon the support of his fellow ops. Besides which, there are a much larger proportion of experienced users on older networks, such as these, who are well aware of the futility of trying to regulate the unregulatable.

It basically comes down to this. Channels die without users. If you have stupid rules and stupid ops, you will get only stupid users, or none at all.

Getting into the 'in-crowd'

Within a group there are usually several different cliques, but they fall into various types. The 'women's knitting club' type, the 'hip and cool with mOnDo spelling group', 'we've been on the Internet for 10 years, so we're God' selection and the 'hugs and kisses, where's my prozac?' emotional hoopla – amongst others (see 'Character Profiling' opposite).

Of course different kinds of people fall into different types of groups, but what is special about cliques is that anyone who doesn't adhere to the principles of the majority of the group feels distinctly out of place, and often there is a 'group attitude' towards the user, rather than each individual having their personal opinions.

Cliques can be very damaging. If you do have a group where everyone has the same opinion then that's not 'A Bad Thing™' (I've yet to find one), but the way that cliques work is that people compromise their opinions to fit in with the rest of a group. The Internet revolves around the issue of 'what people think', and if users simply repeat a belief like it's gospel, then the value of this medium would be severely impaired.

Character Profiling

Trying to slot people into little holes is never that simple, and 'stereotyping', as it is now known, is shunned as being crude and politically incorrect. People aren't really any different on the Net than they are in real life. However, you tend to learn more about them, and you also get a feel for how certain users exhibit particular characteristics.

A little advice

It's often pretty scary how you can read a Dickens novel or watch Harry Enfield on the telly and point out those caricatures and say, 'well that reminds me of Mr X or Mrs Y'.

They might, but remember, even the most shallow-seeming or typical of people often have a lot more to them than is apparent at first.

The other kind of people you meet on IRC, and this is true of real life too, are ones who you can never understand. They infuriate you, irritate you, and yet intrigue you as well. Without these kind of people the world would be a boring place.

This section isn't meant to be insulting to technophiles, geeks, feminists, knitters or long time Internet users. If you find they are, console yourself to the fact that I fit into at least three of the groups.

There follows a list, profiling some of the more common characters you are likely to encounter on IRC. These are gross generalisations, but I hope they will nevertheless arm you with some insight into the traits of users, for future reference.

I've used the Internet for 15 years......

Usually male, these are a fairly rare sort nowadays. This is a peculiar characteristic, and perhaps not a particularly dominant one, but it often crops up, both in real time and delayed response communication.

This type of user tends to reminisce quite a bit and yearn for the MUDs of old. They are often willing to talk at length about how they used to use a FIDONet node, or how they can still recite their first BITNET address.

They are generally an interesting sort, although they whinge about how newbies have swamped 'the place' and how it isn't as good as it used to be. They can be quite unfriendly and require you to prove to them that you aren't 'twink-ish' before they are willing to be civil.

Of course, their need to base arguments upon their 'extensive experience' rather than actual fact does mean that many of them haven't gained much in terms of debating skills, despite their aforementioned wealth of knowledge.

They like:

- technical talk;
- insulting newbies;
- MUDs, being identified as an 'important person', slow modems and old computers, and:
- UNIX.

They **don't** like:

- being told they are wrong;
- the World Wide Web;
- inefficiency;
- coloured text and fancy popups (which look rubbish on old UNIX computers), and;
- Windows 95/98, or anything to do with Microsoft.

Righteous 'knitting-needle' women

This lot can be rather annoying. They are *usually* women – any men who exhibit these characteristics are usually trying to suck up to them.

In their channels they usually spend a great deal of time talking about their husbands or (even worse) their kids, and when given ops they go to extraordinary lengths to protect any children who may accidentally wander onto IRC.

Their channels generally have rather unimaginative names, like '#friendlychat'. Their ability to 'organise' means that their list of channel rules are quite extensive and pedantic, although not as bad as '14 yr old control freak's' (see next item).

Swearing is a big no-no and will only garner you a knitting needle up your backside and a kick out of the channel. They also have these annoying popups which gushingly welcome everyone to the channel, as well as the irritating little quirk that every sentence ends in either 'darling' or 'dear'.

Their technical understanding is usually fairly limited, but they don't like being told they're wrong, particularly by 'youngsters'. I have yet to meet a user who has an effective defence against these creatures as telling them to get lost is rather like telling your gran she's boring. Fortunately there aren't too many of them. Just grin and live with it – they never seem to disappear.

They like:

- children on IRC;
- warm, welcoming and inane channel names and topics, and;
- revolting combinations of coloured text which are known as elaborate popups (usually saying 'hello', welcome back and other such pleasantries).

They **don't** like:

- technical 'stuff';
- liberal-minded weirdos, and;
- swearing or sexual innuendo.

Socially naive 14 year olds

Both of the former groups don't have a great deal of time for this type of character, who either hate him because he is 1) a technological wannabe, with no appreciation for how things were or 2) a young presumptuous 'whippersnapper' who doesn't respect his elders.

They are usually quite easily identified as they have a basic grasp of what constitutes a knowledgable, but most importantly, *respected* netizen. Respect and admiration is after all what they are seeking, but they tend to achieve neither, because they go about it the wrong way.

'In-speak' is usually one of their top priorities, so they spew out cliquey acronyms at a truly incredible rate and do stupid things with their words. One apparently 'trendy' thing to do is to use 'mondo' caps (the name actually comes from a weird and wacky magazine published in San Francisco), which look something like this: 'hEy dONtchA tHinK tHiS roCKs?'

They also like the 'zed effect'. This involves swapping the more traditional pluralising 's' for the less than traditional 'z'. So when you hear the little spotty geeks say 'it rulez', they actually mean 'it rules'. It doesn't really make any more sense, but it's a literal interpretation!

Now the only other way this 'younger generation' is improving the English language is to modify the letter 'c' and metamorphose it into a 'k', usually with some other letter-fiddling along the way. The attempt is to phoneticise netspeak, which is something all of us tend to do – just some people take it a bit far.

Based upon this, 'cool' changes to 'kewl','kool' or 'k3wl', 'cat changes to 'kat'. On the phonetic side of things you have 'ya' instead of 'you', 'cya' instead of 'see you' and lots of other corruptions (take a look at the Netspeak section).

What it basically comes down to is this: many people who are obsessed with technology are rather uncomfortable in social situations, because their scientific 'approach' to life doesn't work well when you come to the very unscientific art of judging people. Usually they learn with age and experience, but being young tends to exacerbate the problem.

The Internet can be a haunt for people who don't really have any friends, which is a fairly sad thing to say, but it is true. 'Youth society' puts great emphasis upon the need to fit in and be 'normal'. To achieve this they try to emulate and be like other people on the Internet, in a rather exaggerated way, but don't have the experience or the perception to get beyond these rather superficial interpretations.

They like:

- pretending to be a technical 'whizz-kid', and;
- being admired, and insulting those who do not fit in.

They **don't** like:

- being told they are immature, and;
- not fitting in, and being the one who is constantly insulted.

'I'm a sophisticated woman'

IRC is full of sexual leering, and when you consider the vast preponderance of males, many women get rather irritated by sexually frustrated nerds (who ALL have pictures which make them look like Arnie) trying to talk them into talking dirty with them.

Tongue twisting aside, the result is that some women, in the belief that all men are like this, try to be equally irritating towards their male counterparts by sneering at them and refusing to hold a meaningful conversation.

There isn't really much more I can add to this, as I'm sure in real life you have a fair experience of members of the opposite sex who can be less than congenial for incomprehensible reasons. The best tactic is to ignore them, and keep your hormones well away from your keyboard, despite the fact that most members of the group are quite good looking. Eventually they will either be reformed or they will disappear; in either event everyone will be better off.

They like:

- talking to like-minded women and dishing the dirt on men, and;
- high flying women, particularly those who work in the media.

They **don't** like:

- sexually frustrated men, and;
- smart men, who might embarrass them. It's probably more accurate to say that they treat the term as an obscure oxymoron.

'I understand a woman's needs'

This is the only type of user that most men find more annoying than the group above.

This select breed of males do not talk to other men, but rather they spend their whole time being gushingly nice to either 1) the 'sophisticated women', which is understandable, as they do present a kind of challenge, or 2) 'knitting club women' which is completely unforgivable.

The result usually follows one of two outcomes. Either 'sophisticated women' fall for their charms, which is pretty rare, because they are rather transparent or they get all the more irate about the immaturity of the male populace.

In the second case, they get treated like some kind of long lost son, which is annoying for every other young male in the channel (and it is primarily young, spotty men who are vying for this attention to fulfil a desire for closeness to women, either in a sexual or maternal sense) who get tarred with the same brush and given the same treatment.

They like:

- women.

They **don't** like:

- other men.

'Liberal-minded weirdos'

The Internet does tend to attract those with strong political views, so on the one side you will find the CND supporters and leftish Greenpeace adherents whilst on the other you find the rabid right-wingers.

Of course their politics is only one aspect of these 'distinguished' characters, but perhaps the most obvious. Whatever their political affiliation they frequently have a very strong belief in free speech and abhor regulation and censorship, which is no bad thing.

This does tend to rather clash with the 'knitting needlers' who see these 'rogues' as the kind of people they wouldn't want their sons and nephews to turn into, although I must admit, the dreadlocks are pretty scary! Due to this they also incur the wrath of their little male minions, for all it is worth.

These libertarians do tend to despise the homely 'feminine men' who they think rather lacking in 'free thought', moral fibre or the various other glorifying synonyms for 'opinions'.

Their attitude to the 'sophisticated woman' varies, although they do have strangely similar opinions to these feminist stalwarts, but as far as men go, these women certainly seem to prefer these type of blokes. Lucky for them.

They like:

- opinionated people, preferably sycophants who agree with them.

They **don't** like:

- regulators, authority and people with strong social affectations, and seemingly no mind of their own.

Truth and Trust

One criticism of the Internet, particularly from parties less than enthused about it, is that you have no idea if the person 'on the other side' is anything like what they proclaim to be.

First of all you have to identify possible motivation for deception. If for example you 'sleep in' and you walk into work late, you surely wouldn't tell your boss 'oh I overslept', but you might say 'the traffic was terribly bad'.

The benefit is that you don't lose your job, whilst on the assumption you don't have a personal relationship with him, the fact that you were deceptive isn't going to make or break friends.

IRC isn't a medium which can be used for financial or similar advantage, although in terms of 'personal gain' it can be considerable. What it comes down to is whether you want someone to like you for what you are.

Fabrication is a time consuming occupation and if they were to find out you were lying, even about a very small thing, then they would undoubtedly wonder whether everything else you say is true.

It sounds rather corny, but there is nothing more destructive to an information based society than misinformation, and in my experience, nothing more valuable than the truth.

Chapter Five

Delayed Response Communication Media

In this chapter we discuss the pros, cons and effects of delayed response communications on the Internet as well as who uses them and why.

Covers

What is it?

As opposed to real-time communication, where there is usually an immediate reply to any message you send, with a delayed response medium such as Usenet you may not get any feedback on what you 'post' for several hours, or even days.

This type of media does, however, have its advantages. Forums such as Usenet are particularly popular in the UK – the colossal phone-bills we receive each month from our friendly high-charging telco act as a deterrent to marathon online IRC sessions.

In addition to this, the amount of time at your disposal enables you to formulate more well considered, researched and informed responses than is possible on a snippety snap medium like IRC.

What you can do is logon to download your news, and post your responses, whilst at the same time do a similar thing with your e-mail and only pay for ten minutes of calls. When offline you can rake through the material to your heart's content for hours and hours, and so avoid a visit from the BT bailiff.

You will often receive much more thoughtful and well conceived answers on Usenet as, firstly, users have more time to formulate a response to a particular argument or question.

Secondly, the potential audience could be hundreds, or in the largest of groups, maybe a thousand users (some readers will never post to a group, but still read it every day) and no-one wants to look ignorant in front of that many people.

A Case of Style

When writing for Usenet or any other medium where you are *broadcasting* (as opposed to IRC or e-mail where you are only writing for a few people) it is expected of you that your grammar and your facts will both be sound.

There is a huge document regularly posted to the newsgroups, *news.answers,* which some may find a little prudish, but which is still probably worth looking at. Written by Jeff Offutt, entitled 'Hints on writing style for Usenet', it is posted every few weeks by Mark Moraes.

Firstly, if you are writing a long and detailed response to an article, quote and reply to each bit of it individually. It will make it much easier to follow, but also don't quote the whole of his post, just the sections you are interested in.

As a general rule, people are much more likely to read your posts and respond to them if they are short (ie, under 60 lines). I remember having an argument with the fantasy author Raymond E Feist, and it took us both a good hour to formulate our 200 line treatises. Not that I cared: his hourly rate is more than mine!

Don't forget, the aim is to enlighten as well as to demonstrate intellectual superiority, so try to explain technical concepts as you go along. Besides which, there is nothing more insulting than explaining something to someone who already understands it.

Use acronyms and abbreviations, but try to define any obscure ones. There is really no excuse not to know them, when there are several net language lexicons on the World Wide Web, as well as a netspeak glossary in this book. Tell them to buy it!

Things to bear in mind

Most Internet writing guides will tell you not to employ some of these techniques or do some of these things, because they will upset people, or even confuse them (which is worse).

I'm not saying that you shouldn't, because the techie types, who are in Internet terms at least as old as the hills, have much more of a taste for clarity and precision than they do for literary flair, but some practices will just make your posts difficult to read and you should be aware of them.

Subtlety is not always communicated well in written form, and it is important to remember that most people who will read your postings won't know you. The same applies to humour as well.

If you've ever read Bill Bryson's page in the Mail 'Weekend' supplement you will realise that not all nationalities have such a finely attuned taste of irony as the British, particularly the Americans, who multiply like rabbits in the online forest.

Smileys :-), frowns :-(, and winks ;-) can sometimes be used to avoid confusions. Have a peek at the smiley glossary in Chapter Three.

Try to make your context clear where the meaning of words may be ambiguous, particularly when technical terms may be involved. For example, if you talk about the importance of 'protocol' or maintaining certain 'standards', then some people may mistake the social definition of the word with the technical interpretation of it. Be warned.

It's much easier to read a mixture of upper and lower case letters, so don't type solely in caps as this is the textual equivalent of SHOUTING AND IT GIVES PEOPLE A HEADACHE!

Leaving out articles such as 'a', 'an', 'the', for the purpose of brevity makes your posts very difficult to read. It is acceptable to a certain extent on IRC and e-mail, but it's not on Usenet. People will just think you're illiterate.

The Internet is an international network.

Nah Nah....we're rocking all over the world

On a final note, it is important to remember that the Internet is an 'international' network. This means that some people's grasp of English might not be very good if they speak it as a second language, and therefore, however funny you may think it to see lots of foreigners poring over their dictionaries looking up your long words, it is a good idea to be selective with your vocabulary.

Bearing in mind that most 'guides to writing on the Net' are written by the same people who crafted those incomprehensible and tedious technical manuals, their advice to keep it simple is boring and to keep it 'clear' is hypocritical.

Combining your flowing prose with the ideas suggested by the 'clear and simple' brigade is not so difficult, and isn't really such a bad idea. Instead of saying 'I am overwhelmed with the exuberance of my verbosity' or 'I talk a lot', you say 'My oral orifice works overtime – I talk a lot'.

There are a few other things new users tend to trip up on. If you specify a time, always specify the time zone as well: GMT or BST in the UK. TV programmes are another great source of confusion. Indeed, the list goes on (for more on this subject, see 'Talking 'Global'' in Chapter Seven), but the moral of the story is ... think about what you write before you send it.

The Art Of Flaming

Flaming or inciting people on Usenet is a much practised pursuit, and there are newsgroups (*alt.flame* being a good example) where it is considered an art form, which is an interesting way of looking at it.

From an ethical viewpoint, insulting people and provoking a clash of personalities instead of thoughtful argument does seem to rather defeat the whole point of Usenet. However, one thing you learn on the Internet is that things don't always have to have a point, providing they are fun.

Just remember, don't 'troll' over people's newsgroups, and only engage in banter with people who look relatively able to defend themselves: although picking on unsuspecting subjects can be enjoyable, it's not very fair and they don't react very well to it. You do have to make a judgement call, but if you read a group for a while, you'll soon get a feel for those who are flame retardant and those who are not.

You may risk being libelled for what you say on the Internet, but it is very rare. If in doubt you could always use an anonymous relay server, through which your actual identity is nigh impossible to establish.

From the beginning

Okay, lesson number one, the first thing you need to know about flaming is that it is an art, not a mass fit of rage. You need to form your words, not from the heat of the moment or from bluster, but work on them like they're a sculpture.

This section offers a rather libertarian approach to the subject. I don't recommend you employ all the tactics herein, but you should be aware of them. If you do go on to use them, don't blame me if you provoke a digital riot!

The Flaming Gospel

1. Feel free to make things up about your opponent. They don't have to be true! Prefix every insult with 'clearly' or 'obviously' or any other word that confirms to the audience your belief that the insult is true – eg, 'Clearly, Jim Jingo is a money grabbing thief of the highest order'.

2. Obviously, assume that everyone wants to hear your flames. From alt.sex.chitua to rec.games.netrek, spread your net wide and enlighten the world.

3. Just because you're paranoid, it doesn't mean they *aren't* after you. There's obviously a conspiracy afoot and you'll do everyone a favour by exposing it.

4. Reverse of #3. Threaten a lawsuit: 'Bilbo Baggins has slated, slandered and (ok, this may be pushing it a bit) sodomised me. See you in court!'

5. Be an armchair 'shrink'. You're a smart person, but more importantly, you did Freud at college. Clearly, you're qualified to psychoanalyse your opponent. For example 'Dennis Dipstick used the word "cucumber" in his post, which clearly indicates his father had bowel problems. On the assumption he has inherited this condition, this would explain why his posts look like dog turds' – animal references are good too.

6. Use foreign phrases. French is good, Latin is fantastic, but Greek is coming into vogue as well. You get two marks for the original form with accreditation, one mark for a translation, plus a Brucie bonus if they have to ask what it means.

Flames that burn bright

Here is the age old, tried-and-tested collection of unmissable classics. It ranges from the verbae of a 'Net cop' to outrageous insults, but either way you're bound to get bombarded with them eventually. (Many thanks to Jorn Barger for help with this.)

Spelling flame

eg: *>> it's a bit of a anakronism*

> I think you'll find that's an 'anachronism'. Your ability to spell is indicative of your level of intelligence in general and of this post in particular. I didn't know four year olds could type!

Pros: they might learn something; it's so pedantic, it's just sooooo cool!

Cons: who cares about spelling; it could be a typo; rather like alcohol, this produces a 'weak flame', which burns out quickly.

A good strategy is to casually fix the error, but maybe a wee bit subtle for some netizens.

Bandwidth wasting flame

eg: *>I think that unless you can display the ability to discuss an Oxford-related topic with some knowledge then I'm afraid people are just going to start ignoring you!*

>>Well, you seldom address any Oxford-related issues, and people never ignore you. On the contrary, they take great care to express their contempt for you every time you give them a chance.

>You must forgive me but I have little access to Oxford local news. That is why I subscribed to alt.oxford.talk in the first place – to get such news. If you could get off my back and stop constantly advertising your porn sites, perhaps I could actually manage to. (And so on...)

Pros: There are plenty of applications for this: they may be in the wrong group or quoting unnecessarily (see 'quoted text' flame) or multi posting instead of cross posting.

Cons: Bandwidth is cheap and by posting a response you may 'waste' bandwidth as well. A vicious circle!

An alternative is to use mail instead of posting the response to Usenet, but flaming is boring without the audience.

Bandwidth variation (quoted text) flame

eg: *>Another irritating little twink feels compelled to repeat 60 lines of a previous message, propagate it around tens of thousands of news servers just so he can add his own little inane comment at the end. Learn to crop, dear boy.*

Pros: People should get in the habit of trimming quotations.

Cons: Same as the previous flame. Although you may stop them doing it again.

The only viable alternative is to use mail instead of posting the response to Usenet, but flaming is boring without the audience. Besides, it fails to 'educate' the lurkers.

The RTFM flame

RTFM stands for, in its most polite form, 'read the flippin' manual'.

Pros: Some people are lazy, and ought to read the newsgroups' FAQs (frequently asked questions).

Cons: Reading manuals is a drag, and they can complain it is too long, out of date, etc, but this one takes a veritable fire engine to damp down.

The problem is that even if you tell them to read the manual/FAQ they probably won't and the helpful thing to do would be to quote the relevant bit, which will make you appear less nasty. Whether that is desirable or not depends on your 'personal objectives'.

You need 'Cloo'

Pros: It's easy, and widely applicable. The insultingly dumb spelling mangle of 'clue' adds extra impact.

Cons: Everyone was a newbie once, and it lacks substance.

You really do need to look for a different angle on this one, because frankly it isn't very original. You can use repetition here to good effect. If you take the newsgroup *demon.service* as a good example, the 'let's upset petulant newbies' clique ends their 'cloo' flames with the phrase '*plonk*'. Supposedly it's the sound of someone being added to a 'killfile'. Or something like that...

'Flaming is pathetic' flame

eg: *>> it's a bit of a anakronism*

> *> I think you'll find that's an 'anachronism'. Your ability to spell is indicative...etc*
>
> *>>It was a typo. All this needless, pedantic flaming just proves there is no reasoning behind your theories.*

Pros: Everyone should stop flaming and we should engage in sensible debate.

Cons: You're probably being hypocritical.

It's rather strange: flamers will go to the lengths of 'your mom is ...' and relating organic matter (carrots, cucumbers, peas and the like) to organs of your body, and yet no flame will incite and frustrate them more than this. It may be acknowledged by a groan or an attack on prudery, but any answer will look pathetic. Great, huh?

Burning out

One of the best ways to burn out a flame is to look up the flamer's record. The invaluable Dejanews (*http://www.dejanews.com)* spares (almost) no-one. What it does is archive everyone's posts (or at least non-binaries) to Usenet, so if five years ago Tom leTit posted a message to *rec.games.tiddlewinks* then you can reveal this embarrassing fact to the whole newsgroup.

'Lurk' in a newsgroup and you will be a better judge of whether flames will be welcomed or not.

If you want to be really meticulous you can look at past flames and see what catches them out, but be warned some die hard flamers put 'X-NoArchive: No' at the bottom of their headers. The result is that you get no meaty past history, indeed you get nowt, because Dejanews doesn't archive these files. Dang!

Golden rule of flaming

The art, and the test, of writing a good flame is summed up quite aptly by Joe Talmadge, in his Flamer's Bible: *'Flames should be witty, insulting, interesting, funny, caustic, or sarcastic, but never, ever, should they be boring'.*

There aren't many newsgroups where users never indulge in a little literary pyrotechnics, but there are some where it is more common, and more acceptable. Be sure to 'lurk' beforehand, to ascertain whether participants will enjoy your flames. In groups such as *rec.games.netrek, demon.service* and *alt.flame,* inciting your opponents is the *mas maoirum.* Flaming is quite an experience, but make sure you buy some asbestos underwear before you try!

E-mail and 'Real Life' Writing

'IRL' stands for 'in real life', which when used on the Internet, refers to everything which isn't.

One of the first things that people notice about communication on the Internet is its informality; this is perhaps e-mail's single-most defining feature.

Try to imagine a good electronic mail as a cross between a telephone conversation and a legible post-it note, and you won't go far wrong. E-mails do not need a 'fancy' composition: you don't usually start an e-mail with 'Dear Mr. Bloggs'. Rather you'd say 'Hello' or 'Good Morning' or dive straight into the subject of your mail. Many people let the information about sender, date, time and subject displayed at the top of the screen do the business of introduction. They just start writing.

E-mail is transmitted often in a matter of minutes, and you do not have to wait for the next post. The informality of an e-mail makes it OK to write, say, a two sentence message to a friend in California – it's no big deal – whereas a letter might come as a surprise and seem too significant (letters seem to encourage us to read between the lines...).

Conversely, if you are e-mailing to someone 'on business' it's advisable to check your spelling and grammar, even if it is a little colloquial. Be aware that not everyone will be quite so well versed in Internet lingo as you will be by the end of this book; make sure the recipient will be able to understand the message at the first reading. People don't like having to have a letter's contents explained to them. Nevertheless, e-mail frees us to some extent from the horrors of letter writing, where many of us are left clueless of *what* and *how* to write by the formal letter-writing conventions we half-learned at school and have long since forgotten. This can often lead to ugly, clanking sentences whose syntax makes them difficult to read and understand.

As with letter writing, though, be sure to include a valid e-mail return address and possibly a telephone number as well. If you've configured your e-mail client properly, when the recipient hits the 'reply' button it should pop up with your address (the 'Sender:' and 'Reply-To': headers will have this information).

Just as you might sign a letter with your name, you can include a digital 'signature' to personalise your e-mails. My business one looks like this:

--
Josh Smith – Media and Technology Freelance Journalist
e: josh@computerstep.com – p: +44 0 1926 817999
'Externals may change, but man does not.'

. . . . .Cicero

The '-- ' bit at the beginning is called a signature separator. In the form 'DASH-DASH-SPACE-RETURN' it separates the signature from the main body of your message. The advantage is that functional newsreaders and e-mail clients will chop the signature off when they quote the post in the return message. You should include one – it is a small distinguishing feature included by those who know something about the Internet and its absence will be noted by the more pedantic of Internet old-timers. The signature shouldn't be a total of more than 4 lines long, excluding the separator (some software, notably Microsoft's Outlook Express, strips the trailing space, no matter how hard you try to 'do things properly'. Complain to Bill Gates!)

E-mail also compares favourably with voice telephone calls and faxes: the person you are calling has to be at home or in the office at exactly the time you call. An e-mail doesn't have to interrupt something – instead it waits in its mailbox to be read. Answer machines are difficult to talk to while fax machines are often busy – plus e-mail does not degenerate as it gets passed along the telephone line, because it is made up of digitally encoded characters.

Phone calls are often thought of as more personal, but in reality, conversations must follow mutually agreed guidelines if long and uncomfortable pauses are to be avoided. With e-mail, there is no pressure to respond instantly and no sense, from a tone of voice, that the other person would rather be elsewhere. E-mail allows you to compose your thoughts logically and concisely whilst managing still to convey a sense of spontaneity. For all these reasons, e-mail is an excellent form of communication.

Newsgroup Hierarchy

With over 30,000 newsgroups currently available on a server with a full 'feed' it makes sense to organise them into groups so it's easy for people to find what they want.

It is important to note that, unlike a web page, a newsgroup doesn't exist on 'one site'. It is present on tens of thousands of news servers around the world (assuming a full distribution).

There are a huge number of top level hierarchies (for a list of the most popular ones, see page 13). In addition to this there are hundreds of other, rather more obscure groups like the pl.* hierarchy, dedicated to the discussion of Polish issues. Riveting.

Binaries

Binaries are not text files, they are pictures or executables (programs).

Binaries, such as picture files, are almost exclusively posted to the *alt.** hierarchy, mainly in a sub group called *alt.binaries.**. Because of the haphazard nature of the *alt* groups, they aren't as well organised as the 'Big 7', which were the original seven hierarchies formed soon after Usenet was formed. Another top level hierarchy, 'humanities', has been added, so this group is now known as the 'Big 8'.

Traditionally, *'alt'* groups are looked upon as lower quality newsgroups compared to those in the mainstream hierarchies, and are host to less traffic. This is, however, not always true, with *alt.usage.english* having thousands of articles in it at any one time (articles expire usually every two weeks or so, server dependent) and *alt.writing* is considered, by its participants at least, to be a better group than *misc.writing*. So the generalisations that were valid five or six years ago aren't always today. What is true though, is that the alt hierarchy tends to suffer from poorer propagation than the 'Big 8'.

Newsgroup creation

How you create a newsgroup depends on the hierarchy which you want to create it in. Of course, the ultimate decision of whether to carry a group or not lies with the 'admin' (administrator) of each individual server, but in the past they haven't had time to vet 30,000 newsgroups, so they 'honoured' all control messages which came their way. When you consider the prohibitive expense of providing a Usenet feed, admins are becoming a little more choosy, often only adding 'alt' groups upon special request.

A control message is usually posted to the relevant group; *alt.config* for the *'alt'* groups. The main distinction between the *'alt'* groups and other hierarchies is that you don't need a newsgroup proposal backed by a majority vote, and in theory you can simply whoosh off a properly formatted control message (this is important, else some news admins will ignore it) and you'll have your group. For this reason you tend to get a lot of empty groups in the *'alt'* hierarchy, although Usenet spam often makes it desirable for newsgroup participants to switch groups to avoid the commercial verbae.

Management for the Big 8 hierarchy is contained within the *'na'* groups, *news.admin.**. They usually have a rather heavy message load – be warned!

Other Notables

The *n.a.n-a.** (*news.admin.net-abuse.**) groups deal with network abuse, including Usenet spam and UCE (Unsolicited Commercial E-mail).

Cancel messages, issued on Usenet spam and articles posted in error, are found in the *control* and *control.cancel* groups. If you post articles and they don't turn up, you can look to see if anyone has cancelled them, inadvertently or otherwise. A clever little thing called 'Dave the Resurrector' can be used to recall posts that are killed off without good reason. Unfortunately it only works in the *n.a.n-a.** hierarchy.

Another quirk which befuddles new users are *'.d'* groups – eg, you have one group called *alt.stories* and another called *alt.stories.d.* So what is the difference? The 'root' group contains the stories or the BASIC code whilst the *'.d'* group contains discussion relating to the main group. So people who want to read the stories or survey the coding, but don't want to read the comments passed upon them don't have to. You see, some things on Usenet *do* make sense.

Chapter Six

Argument, Discussion and Debate

The Internet is primarily a network for the transmission and exchange of information. In this chapter we discuss the most popular and lively means by which this is achieved.

Covers

Internet 'One-upmanship'

Debate on the Internet is undoubtedly of the confrontational variety. The idea is that the strongest argument wins, but inevitably this is not always the case as the success of an argument is as much dependent on the persuasiveness of its supporters as it is on its innate strength.

It is important to realise that the aim of participators in discussion forums such as Usenet and the WELL isn't to find the right answer: rather, it is to prove that their answer is right.

Together with the art of flaming, the practice of Internet one-upmanship is useful – nay essential – to understand if you are to be successful in online debate.

Of course this concept isn't something sprung from the digital primaeval soup of the early Internet. It's a skill practised throughout most people's lives, and demonstrated quite aptly in Stephen Potter's book, 'Potter on Lifemanship'. His response to one-upmanship, or lifemanship as he calls it, is undoubtedly better than mine.

> *'In one of the unpublished notebooks of Rilke there is a phrase which might be our text: " . . . if you're not one up you're . . . one down" To be one up you must make the other man feel like something has gone wrong. The Lifeman is never caddish himself, but how simply, and certainly, often, he can make the other feel a cad, and over prolonged periods.'*

Glaciation

Of course you may find it rather curious as to how all this works out online, and how exactly the theory of one-upmanship can be distinguished from mere flaming. First of all a *Lifeman*, to use Potter's term, should always be congenial, which differs quite profoundly from a flamer who is always a sharp pin. The idea is that you damage the other person's *dignitas* by enhancing (or at the very least, whilst maintaining) your own.

Glaciation is when someone does something to provoke a response, and you do nothing in return. The opposite of the effect they desire. If someone tells a funny story, you should not laugh or smile, indeed you should do nothing at all. This is easy on the Internet, if less effective, but if a user continually posts to a newsgroup or says something on a channel, yet garners no response, it not only makes him feel uneasy but also it makes him feel unwelcome.

A more inflammatory gesture towards this individual would not be as effective and reflect badly upon the gesticulator. It also gives the presumably innocent victim something to respond to, which will undoubtedly strike a chord with the more righteous members of the group.

Technical prowess

If you happen to be technically proficient with computers, then luring an opponent out of his subject of technological expertise is an excellent idea. Of course, what you want to do first is to alienate him from other sections of the group, so that they storm in, torches blazing, to pick him up on his mistake.

Many technophiles find it hard to distinguish between technical knowledge and intelligence.

Of course it may be completely unrelated to the argument you have with him, but it will suffice in allowing you to doubt his credentials. You can then propose, in a sneaky, quiet sort of way, that your argument is not only right because of X, Y and Z, but because you are supporting it and you have greater technical or intellectual credence. You do have to remember that many technophiles on the Net find it hard to distinguish between technical knowledge and intelligence – strange but true.

Group one-upmanship

Enacting a plan like this is obviously difficult, but you can also gain 'cred' for yourself by forming a clique, and this is the prevalent form of one-upmanship on the Internet. It's also, not surprisingly, the easiest.

This is based upon the human premise that everyone thinks you're right so you must be. Rather like a choir, having ten people in the same room singing from the same hymn sheet sounds a lot better than a hundred people around the world singing slightly different songs at different times, in different places. At most you're only going to hear one of these people singing at a time, and in a metaphysical sense their vocalisation seems to be weaker. The theory is that if you tell someone that something is true enough times, then they will believe it, and it certainly seems to work online.

Take for example, a scenario such as this. Person A says something which is smart, and Person B and Person C don't say anything but are quietly impressed with Person A's comment.

Person D says lots of stupid things in a newsgroup, flames left, right and centre and generally gets on everyone's nerves. Eventually Person D says something which is rather sensible and Person A attacks it. Rather than agreeing with Person D the rest of the newsgroup sides with Person A. They don't really understand the argument, but Person A seems like a 'decent chap' and sensible so they support him.

As you can see, this collaboration isn't carefully constructed and discussed over tea and biscuits in a WI meeting. Often it falls together as a result of luck and human bonding, but sometimes it can be engineered to an extent. If you can engineer it to your favour it can be much to your advantage and useful in future engagements.

So what's the point?

The point is that Usenet and other debate mediums have the unfortunate affliction that their participants tend to judge arguments not on their actual quality, but the apparent quality and public appraisal of those who support them.

On another note, flaming and one-upmanship are similar in many respects, but the aim of the former is undoubtedly to entertain, whilst the aim of the latter is sly coercion to improve general public opinion of oneself. Which is undeniably destructive to what Usenet is all about.

Talking Technical

As I mentioned two pages previously, baffling your opponent with technical talk is a sure way to gain the upper hand. Of course, this isn't always possible. For example, interjecting with RIPE's new proposals for the issuing of IP addresses in a discussion concerned with Zionism isn't going to get you very far. Nevertheless, most newsgroups or IRC channels have a large proportion of participants with some technical background.

Of course anything will work...

Technical baffling is by far and away the most popular form of belittling, because technical knowledge is something which is greatly respected on the Internet. You do have to remember, though, that strolling into a Christian group and showing a thorough knowledge of the Bible would undoubtedly garner you praise, but doing the same in a Hindi forum would only receive sneers, contempt or as we have already learnt is even worse, no response whatsoever.

You need to think about what kind of people read and post to the group, to ascertain exactly what kind of input they appreciate. That's why reading *all* the articles in a group can put you at a distinct advantage, as opposed to just reading those threads which you have contributed to.

Tips for success 1 – RFCs (Request For Comment)

RFC stands for 'Request For Comment'.

If discussing a technical point make sure you read all the RFCs on the subject. It's a real conversation stopper. *'There's no law that says mail has to be delivered that way!'* could aptly be responded to with: *'but RFC blah blah blah says that it does!'*

At this point, anyone who understands what RFCs do knows that it is useless to argue. Internet old timers view them with a veneration which is only hardened by the fact that Microsoft ignores them all the time.

They also have a deep appreciation for anyone who can dig them up, because there are almost 2500 of the darn things, half of which are nearly antiques and they are boring as hell to read.

RFC stands for Request for Comment. In the olden days, people used to propose standards, but not everyone got to see them and approval was a very decentralised business. What eventually happened was that standards were suggested, and once input had been made, and as time passed, they became 'accepted'. Approved through the lack of unresolved objection, many have been adopted by ISO, ANSI and other standards organisations.

Although the RFCs were sometimes updated, they were held in great reverence by traditionalists who appreciated the way they had been fairly agreed upon – very non-combative and fair. Don't mistake their undefinitive name for an undefinitive nature: to technical people, if there is a 'law' on the Internet, this is it.

Take a look at this site. It has the full listing, and fortunately there is an index – use it!

- Demon's RFC list

  ftp://ftp.demon.co.uk/pub/doc/rfc/

Tips for success 2 – language

If you want to confuse (which is good from a one-upmanship perspective, because they might interpret it wrongly) or merely make them feel inferior, then using a technical term when a simple one will suffice never ceases to really upset them.

'Convo' is short for conversation.

For example, rather than talking about TCP/IP, which most people will know about, fling 'Transmission Control Protocol' and 'Internet Protocol' into the convo. They might not recognise it.

Remember, digression can be good. Everyone likes a bit of technical trivia. Obscure a very simple topic with lots of irrelevant information about peripheral issues; so if you make a simple point about TCP/IP don't forget to explain, *in detail,* the technical nuances of UDP (basically Internet Protocol either works with TCP or UDP – they are different methods of transferring data between computers).

Always pick up on little language errors which might demonstrate a lack of understanding. For example if they refer to TCP/IP as '*a*' protocol do not forget to remind them, in the sweetest, most sickly and helpful way possible (nasty piece of work, aren't I?) that it is in fact *two* protocols and should thus be referred to as a *protocol suite*.

Pedants are great. The Internet is an absolute mine of useless information which the people who use it love, and nothing annoys someone more than being picked up by a pedantic, preaching troll.

Tips for success 3 – Traceroutes and other falsifiable stuff . . .

When all else fails, when the newsgroup *vox populi* start to lose faith in your argument and you realise you are onto a dud runner, you can always make it up.

The technical community has a great affinity with statistics. This is rather peculiar when you consider how frequently they are 'produced' by less than scientific means, within that group's cloisters.

A 'traceroute' or 'tracert' (the name of the program under DOS) is kind of like a detailed ping reply. A 'ping' will tell you how far, in electronic terms, you are from a specific place, but a 'tracert' will tell you which route that ping takes, and the specifics of each leg of the journey. A tracert utility is supplied by default with Windows.

The situations in which they can become useful are numerous. Let us say, for instance, you use an IRC server and you whinge and moan about the lag, to which they respond with the age old cliche: *'it must be your ISP's fault!'*

Unfortunately the results from your traceroute, as seen over the page (which, incidentally, although the route is accurate, I just made up the results – Demon has good routing generally) confirm this to be the case.

What needs to be enacted is a slight modification, a little tweak, a small adjustment – I'll spare you the details. The three columns show the results of three different test packets, the result being that an average of those will give a fair indication of the speed of the link.

```
C:\WINDOWS>tracert london.uk.eu.kewl.org
Tracing route to london.uk.eu.kewl.org [195.8.71.10]
over a maximum of 30 hops:
 1  350 ms  426 ms  377 ms  finch-198.access.demon.net
 2  218 ms  299 ms  296 ms  finch-core-1-fxp3.router.demon.net
 3  147 ms  144 ms  134 ms  ash-fxp0.router.demon.net
 4  128 ms  127 ms  130 ms  linxgw1.netkonect.net [195.66.224.18]
 5  133 ms  136 ms  127 ms  docgw14.netkonect.net [194.62.47.8]
 6  126 ms  127 ms  124 ms  clara-gw.netkonect.net [194.164.70.26]
 7  140 ms  145 ms  137 ms  london.uk.eu.kewl.org [195.8.71.10]
```

A desirable change here would be to made Claranet's link to its provider (Netkonnect) look really bad, so we can turn around and say *'Ah, I have to disagree. These results clearly indicate that your server's connection to the network is broken.'* As a general note, using the word 'broken' is a brilliant idea. Of course, it isn't broken, rather it's a bit slow, but there's no harm in exaggerating.

The results you share with your beloved cyber buddies should look something like this.

```
C:\WINDOWS>tracert london.uk.eu.kewl.org
Tracing route to london.uk.eu.kewl.org [195.8.71.10]
over a maximum of 30 hops:
1  125 ms  128 ms  127 ms  finch-198.access.demon.net
2  127 ms  129 ms  126 ms  finch-core-1-fxp3.router.demon.net
3  147 ms  144 ms  134 ms  ash-fxp0.router.demon.net
4  128 ms  127 ms  130 ms  linxgw1.netkonect.net [195.66.224.18]
5  133 ms  136 ms  127 ms  docgw14.netkonect.net [194.62.47.8]
6  288 ms  261 ms  256 ms  clara-gw.netkonect.net [194.164.70.26]
7  412 ms  462 ms  450 ms  london.uk.eu.kewl.org [195.8.71.10]
```

How things progress from there will depend on how savvy your opponent is. Undoubtedly, when you produce the results, group confidence will take an almighty swing in your favour, but it's more than likely your opposite number will perform a traceroute for themselves, and their results will be different.

This causes problems. You can accuse them, in the most friendly of ways, of lying completely or maybe being incapable of operating a simple program like traceroute.

It is wise to make sure that no-one who uses your ISP reads the particular newsgroup in question else they could perform a similar route report, and the resulting evidence would be much to your disadvantage.

Your only recourse then would be to blame your results on a 'momentary blip in network operation' (tech jargon for things were a bit weird when I was doing my test), and retreat from the discussion with your ego only mildly impaired. It was an honest mistake, wasn't it? Yeah, right.

Constructive or Destructive

One-upmanship is bad. Although it generally stands that smart people propose smart ideas and those who appear to back idiotic ones continue to do so, there are exceptions to the rule.

In a blatantly puritanical sense, Usenet isn't about people or arguments, rather it is a tool for the divination of the truth. Practising flaming or one-upmanship only obscures this goal, which is A Bad Thing™.

In the former case I believe that the 'fun and entertainment' factor is fairly admissible, but the only pleasure derived from one-upmanship is the knowledge and intellectual satisfaction that you've manipulated everyone something rotten. Which is a bit sad and pathetic.

The question you have to ask yourself before you send a Usenet post winging its way across the world is whether it is, on aggregate, 'constructive' (in that it adds some useful evidence or insight to the argument), 'destructive' (in that it unfocusses everyone from the real source of debate) or 'pointless and relatively harmless' (into which category witticisms and mild jibes gravitate).

The moral of the story is to think about what you write *before* you send it. A misjudged poke or a tame insult can sometimes backfire, and come back to haunt you later on.

Chapter Seven

Network Etiquette

Network Etiquette, more commonly known as 'Netiquette', is a way of using the Internet which is generally agreed to result in the least amount of conflict, and is the gospel regarding appropriate behaviour online.

Covers

What are FAQs?

FAQs are Frequently Asked Questions, which are designed to help users new to a particular piece of software, network, topic or group to understand it better.

Most newsgroups have an FAQ, some IRC channels have an FAQ and there is explanatory documentation on every subject from aardvarks to lock-picking to zoology.

FAQs come in three basic 'flavours', and these are explored below.

FAQs with questions

This is the original McCoy with an index of questions at the beginning, and the body of the text comprising of various questions, usually preceded by the letter 'Q' and answers following in close pursuit, preceded by the letter 'A' – such originality!

RTFM stands for 'Read the Flippin' Manual' – or FAQ!

The disadvantage of this format is that it is difficult and time consuming to arrange the questions in any meaningful order of progression or group them according to subject type. For this reason, mainly small, very subject specific FAQs are written in this format.

FAQs without questions

Despite being a bit of a misnomer, these probably comprise well over two thirds of the FAQs on the Internet. Rather than providing a likely list of Q&As the idea is that a document such as this should answer any basic questions you have. Sometimes it is appended with the more traditional idiot's guide, discussed above.

This format is much more suitable for acquiring an in-depth understanding of a topic, and is often accompanied by a suitably lexical table of contents, which makes the document easier to navigate. For this reason many FAQs, traditionally written in plain text, have been converted to HTML (web page language) to make it easier to flick from the table of contents to the section indicated by the hyperlink. Try to find the web enhanced version – it makes it a lot easier to navigate your way through a document.

Meta-FAQs

Due to the vast plethora of explanatory documentation, there is often a need to index the material, so that the people who want to find it can. Pseudo-FAQs do just that. They are frequently posted to newsgroups because they are considerably smaller than the documents they reference, avoiding the message kludge which can be rather annoying when you download a lot of Usenet material, and because of their small size they are easy to maintain. The links should always be up to date.

And other FAQ related wotsits?

Some groups and IRC channels offer documents called Ds&Ds, known to normal humans as 'Do's and Don'ts'. They are exceedingly definitive, usually short and fairly useful pieces of information to ingest.

FOCS files are also becoming more popular, particularly in games related groups. It stands for 'Frequently Offered Clever Suggestions'. Before you have any great ideas to improve something, it is usually wise to read the FOCS document, which will tell you the result last time it was suggested or implemented, how and why it did or didn't work and other relevant information. Of course it doesn't mean you can't suggest it again, providing you attempt to address the issues highlighted in the FOCS.

Where can I find them?

The first place to look for FAQs is *news.answers,* a newsgroup which carries bucket loads of documentation for newsgroups. Some of the files are multi-part and quite massive, so should give you enough bedtime reading for several nights. It can take an age to download, so you might be well advised to try some FAQ archives first, such as those listed below. FAQs pertaining to individual groups are usually posted on a monthly cycle to the group in question.

- *http://www.faqs.org/*
- *ftp://ftp.uu.net/usenet/news.answers/*

Talking 'Global'

It sounds like a BT advertising slogan enticing us to spend more time with a telephone glued to our ears, but nay, it's much more than that.

Although by some philosophical accounts 'people are the same, the world over', it is important to realise there is a skill in communicating effectively with people whose culture may be very different from your own.

The British by all accounts have a rather peculiar sense of humour which together with their overly ironic traits can result in misinterpretation of what they say. Use humour with caution and be aware of your audience.

Words to be wary of – across the pond

Aside from the difficulty of people speaking different languages, there are still numerous opportunities for poor communication due to a lack of cultural understanding. It is true, in my experience, that foreigners know a lot more about the US than Americans know about foreign countries.

When you consider that Americans make up well over half of all Internet users, it pays to be familiar with Oscar Wilde's wise words on the Anglo-American divide: 'Two nations divided by a common language.'

When talking about academia, bear in mind that a public school in the States is not a private sector institution as it is in the UK, and that they may not know what a Primary or Secondary school is, let alone the differences between Higher and Further education. Use such terms with care – or with explanation.

If you state a price you should always state definitively the currency it is measured in. Instead of writing *'it cost about £10'* or even worse *'it cost about ten quid'* (slang can trip people up as well), you should write *'it cost about 10ukp'*.

UKP stands for UK pounds. If you are particularly helpful you could state the price in dollars as well, usually expressed as USD – US dollars.

International Awareness

Despite the xenophobic qualities of the British, no-one can top the average American who seems to think that the White House is the centre of the world and everything either side of the Atlantic and Pacific, north of Niagara and south of Juarez is like some kind of jungle or desert or such like.

UKP=UK pounds; GBP=Great Britain pounds. Although less common it is the ISO standard. USD=US dollars.

You do have to show a little patience though, and unlike the British who despite being unable to win at cricket, rugby or football,. still seem quite convinced that they are the best at everything, the American view of the world is obscured by the cultural 'hugeness' of their own country, not necessarily by their own self importance.

Incidentally, you'll find that it is Canadians who whinge incessantly about American money (two types of dollar in one continent can be confusing), the English who whinge incessantly about American spelling and their obsession with Webster, and with Strunk & White's guide to minimalist writing rather than adherence to those age-old tomes of the OED and Fowler's Modern English Usage.

Meanwhile, the French as usual complain about their food and their McDonalds and their wines, and anything else which the Canadians and English have left behind . . . and then there are the Russians – but that's another story.

National Flames

The American dominance of the Internet can be a little peeving, but let me assure you there is nothing more pathetic than 'my country is better than your country' flames, particularly when you consider the likely winner through sheer numbers.

People from other countries can be very interesting, and cultivating a friendship with them can be worthwhile. If you ever go abroad, it can save on hotel bills as well!

Being Topical

Most newsgroups are subject orientated, with *misc.misc* excepted. The expedience with which they keep to their 'remit', if such a term is suitable, varies from group to group.

Bear in mind that the purpose with which some groups are created may not be immediately apparent. For example, *demon.service* is a newsgroup designed (according to its charter) *'to be a place where users can let off steam',* whilst many people in the newsgroup seem of the distinct impression that it is a group to discuss Demon's service provision – as do Demon Internet's official magazine, Demon Dispatches.

You can talk about anything in *'d.s'* (as it is commonly known), and although it is usually concerned with Demon's level of service, whinges tend to garner more interesting responses than compliments.

IRC Channels

These do not always specify topics of conversation, although, clearly, *#html* is more likely to discuss web page design than wet nursing. What are more common are channels which forbid the discussion of certain topics, some which may be slightly surprising.

For example, *#england* on Dalnet doesn't allow people to talk about football, because it is, in fact, run by a bunch of elderly American ladies who aren't really interested in the subject.

As a general rule, however, making certain subjects *verboten* because you don't relish the discussion of them is bad form, particularly when you consider that the views held by the channel operators do not always reflect those of channel participants in general. This is often the case on services networks such as Dalnet and Undernet where the administrations of popular channels are allowed to stagnate.

Attributions

When you consider the vast amount of material contributed by authors into the public domain, it is not surprising that some of them get a little ratty when work isn't properly attributed to them.

When you quote directly from a source you should always make it clear what is what *you* have written and what is from another source. In the case of one or more sources being employed, the two should be distinguishable.

It is common practice to ask the author's permission before quoting material, although this isn't really necessary. It is necessary, however, to include the author's name next to the quoted material, followed by an asterisk and, appended to the end of the document, his or her e-mail address (if available), the document from which the material is quoted and a link to that document if it is archived online. An ISBN, a number which is used to identify books (or an ISSN in the case of magazines), can be useful for persons who wish to view the material in greater depth.

Something like this would be fairly typical:

Many people write for the Net out of the goodness of their hearts – at least give them credit for it.

In his book, *PCs in easy steps*, published by Computer Step, Harshad Kotecha said that, '*It is a common fallacy that upgrading a PC must be left to professionals*'. *(Kotecha, p161, ed.4, harshad@computerstep.com)*

ISBN 1-874029-90-3

It's also much more useful to anyone who looks at it to find what you have quoted in print, because as we know from our discussion on one-upmanship, misquoting can be rife.

From what I've said, you know that Harshad Kotecha is the author (and you know his e-mail address), Computer Step is the publisher, the material is on p161 in the 4th edition (page numbers do vary between editions) and if you type the ISBN into an online catalogue (such as *http://www.bookpages.com*) you will be able to get further information about the text. Marvellous huh?

Cross Posting and Multi Posting

We have already heard about how cross posting is used for annoying advertising purposes on Usenet, but sometimes cross posting one message to several groups can be desirable. This must meet two criteria:

a) Is anyone in the target group interested in reading what you have to say?

b) Is the subject matter similar to that specified by either
    i) the newsgroup moderator (in moderated groups);
    ii) the group FAQ, or;
    iii) the newsgroup control message/charter?

The distinction between these two questions isn't obviously apparent. The issue is that participants in, let's say, *uk.school.secondary.teachers* might well be interested in information regarding the status of HNDs as higher education qualifications, as they all would have degrees, but it is not relevant to the group – it should not be posted.

In addition to this, it is essential that you should personally read all the groups you are cross posting to, if you initiate the thread. In my opinion (some users might disagree with this) when following up to a cross posted article you should continue the thread in all the groups where the topic seems vaguely relevant. Thread discontinuity can be very annoying, so leave it up to the people either in the individual groups or the person who initialised the cross posting to change the newsgroup or follow up headers.

Headers

Each newsgroup post has information before the body text which tells the news server and makes available to other clients information such as your e-mail address, the newsgroups the document was posted to, and such like.

Two very important headers are the 'newsgroup' and 'follow-up' lines. The newsgroup header lists which groups the document is posted to, whilst the follow up line contains the default setting for any follow up to your post, with regard to where the next post is sent. If you change this header it is important you inform any readers in the main body of your article, as many users don't read the headers of every, or indeed, any post.

What is the difference between 'cross posting' and 'multi posting'?

Needlessly cross posting material is frowned upon, because it is annoying rather than because it is particularly resource hungry. What has to be understood is that when more than one newsgroup is entered in the newsgroup line, the file may be downloaded by the participants of more than one newsgroup, but only one copy of the post is stored on the news server.

Another method of spanning a wide range of newsgroups is multi posting. This is far more intensive as far as resource usage goes. This is typically employed by commercial newsgroup spammers. In this case a separate article is posted to each newsgroup, although the content of each article is usually the same, the idea is that it is harder to cancel ten or twenty messages than it is one message cross posted to ten or twenty groups. You should NEVER intentionally multipost, firstly because it is network abuse and secondly because any follow ups to the post will not be linked, making a substantial discussion unlikely.

So how many groups should I cross post to?

Well there is no definite answer to this question, although generally five is quite enough. Although we mentioned criteria before, try to get used to the idea that you should post to Usenet not to obtain recognition and give you something to respond to, but because you feel you have some information or query to contribute which you think might interest the readers of all the groups – yourself included.

Do's and Don'ts for Usenet

Over the next few pages are some of the Do's and Don'ts for Usenet that haven't been fully covered thus far in the book. There aren't many hard and fast rules on the Net, but there shouldn't be many exceptions to these.

The Do's

DO use your common sense. People pretty much act, respond and feel the same as they do in real life. If you apply the same standards to your behaviour online as you do offline (murderers, robbers, arsonists and lawyers excepted) you shouldn't go far wrong.

DO learn how to use your newsreader properly. Ensure that the line length in your articles does not exceed 78 characters. Try not to post multiple copies of the same article.

DO employ humour and wit in your posts, but try not to be offensive to other people – particularly foreigners, who may have different cultural standards to your own.

DO quote when following up articles, but quote only the relevant bits. A '>' sign preceding each line of quotation is the standard identification for such material. Ensure that all material is correctly attributed, and in the case of material taken from sources other than the current thread that the information specified in 'Attributions' in this chapter is included in your post.

DO include a disclaimer on your articles if you are posting from a business account to indicate whether or not you are speaking on behalf of your company.

DO use a signature if you feel it appropriate, but it is advisable to insert a 'sig separator' at the beginning of the signature, which looks like this: '-- ' (DASH-DASH-SPACE-RETURN) and also to make sure that the signature is no more than 4 lines long.

DO specify a valid e-mail address with ALL your posts.

DO listen. 'Don't be a dipstick: play it by ear.'

The Don'ts

DON'T flame excessively and try not to pick on the 'weaker' members of the group, who everyone else uses as flame bait. Consider the old adage: *'pick on someone your own size!'*

DON'T cross post gratuitously.

DON'T post 'large' (over 10k) binaries to Usenet, and only post binaries to groups specified for that purpose.

DON'T hold discussions in groups which have a subgroup identified with the letter *'d'* (eg, comp.basic.code and comp.basic.code.d), and vice versa – don't post code extracts to discussion groups.

DON'T litter your post with literary affectations, intercaps or Mondo-esque spellings. iT jUsT aiN'T kEwL!

DON'T witter on. Try to keep your posts succinct and under a hundred lines.

DON'T fight a losing argument. Sometimes it's best to cut your losses and admit you were wrong.

DON'T start an argument you can't finish. If you are going on holiday the day after you flame everyone, you won't be able to respond.

DON'T start an argument you can't win. If you don't have a technical background don't debate technical subjects.

DON'T be boring. If you must make an attack, *ad hominem* and *ad nauseam*, DON'T make it *ad infinitum* as well.

DON'T say things you might later regret. Assume permanence and ubiquity.

DON'T respond in anger. If you must flame, construct it coolly, carefully and concisely. Remember, it's an art form.

DON'T be timid. Waggle your newsreader at some groups and join in – Usenet is as good as the people who use it.

Do's and Don'ts For IRC

Here is a similar thing to the page before, except this collection of "aye's and nay's" relates to IRC and similar real time communication media.

The Do's

DO read what you write before you send it, and be aware of your audience.

DO use emoticons such as <grin> or *smile* as well as smileys such as :-) or ;-P, but do so sparingly.

DO learn how to use and manage your IRC client, and make sure you send the right messages to the right channels – otherwise things can get confusing.

DO message people, but don't complain if they don't say anything. They might be away from their computer, playing Quake, too busy talking to someone else or maybe they just don't want to talk to you. Either way, it's their choice.

DO greet people when they enter a channel, but don't set up an automated 'greeter' which messages everyone as they enter the channel. It's impersonal and rather lame.

DO set yourself 'away', or change your nick to reflect your absent state if you are going to the loo, raiding the fridge or otherwise going to be elsewhere for more than a few minutes.

DO be helpful to new users. Conversely, don't be afraid to ask old time propeller-heads for help.

DO try to be gregarious, but expect the same in return. If someone asks you kindly to stop using a nickname, because it is their regular handle, then it would be polite to do so, but there are a surprising number of people on the Internet who are as rude as hell. In which case, you can tell them to get lost, or any other words to that effect which take your fancy.

DO what thou wilt. There are only a few hard and fast rules for what to do and not to do on IRC, but there is no greater tool for social acceptability than common sense – use it!

The Don'ts

DON'T try to be someone you are not. Make people like you, for what you are, rather than for what you want them to think you are.

DON'T harass people.

DON'T get involved with IRC politics. It is puerile, pathetic, but most of all it's pointless – it's just IRC after all.

'Channel operators' and 'opers' are people who manage channels and networks respectively.

DON'T hassle channel operators for 'ops'.

DON'T hassle network administrators for O:lines (operator status.) Remember they are volunteers, so be kind and appreciative of the time they give, and don't swear at them when they can't help you.

DON'T complain excessively about channel rules or policies. If you don't like them, go somewhere else.

DON'T try to maliciously take over channels or flood users.

DON'T say anything that you wouldn't like to be quoted on. Many people log all their personal and public conversations.

DON'T join more channels than you can possibly read.

DON'T lurk in channels unless you're a channel regular. Some people can be offended if they talk to you but you don't respond.

DON'T be pedantic about netiquette. In my opinion, complaining about being offended by anything on the Internet is bad form. If you don't like it, don't read it. Simple.

DON'T, if you ever have the misfortune to run your own channel, have stupid rules which kick people out for swearing, disagreeing with channel operators, peeing on the founder's virtual cornflakes, etc. Consistency is everything. If you ever find such a channel, (and it's not difficult) take my advice – leave it!

How and When to Complain

One of the things you learn in real life as much as you do on the Internet is that knowing *when* to do things is as important as knowing *how* to do things.

Every so often it pays to refer to pearls of wisdom somewhat shinier than your own. Internet guru, Michael Lawrie, named the Information Super Highwayman by Internet Magazine, and founder of IRC Net, had something rather interesting to say on the subject of complaining and netiquette.

This was posted to the newsgroup *demon.local* during the autumn of 1995.

"Meanwhile, the rot is really setting in isn't it. Look at IRC, people who were once sane now want their pound of flesh whenever someone annoys them. If someone new came onto a channel in the past and annoyed people, it would be pretty much ignored, folks may kick them off and ban them, but that was about the limit. Now people want to mail their site master, and failing that their domain masters – What on earth has gotten in to you? Do you honestly think for one moment that the domain masters care what someone says on IRC? And what if that someone is a student and gets thrown out of university because of your (more than likely heated, and overly exaggerated) complaint. Would you be proud of that? Do you like to ruin people's lives because they make mistakes? Is it worth it? If you have genuine complaints use proper channels. If you don't know what the proper channels are, ask someone who does. We don't lynch people any more in the real world, why should we on IRC?

News? I haven't read it for years really. I was a newsmaster for a major site once, I had to, and apart from the antics of groups like alt.flame, most of the groups were at least civilised. Sure there were arguments, sometimes they got personal but never in my experience did they stoop to the levels that are becoming more and more common every day. I guess I have to refer to the postings between Paul Allen and Paola Kathuria on this group. I like a good gossip, I am well known for it. But this isn't gossip, this is malicious, libelous, uncivilised and primitive warfare, there is no place for it, it is plain rude. No-one gains anything, everyone loses something.

Why are you all so confrontational? I wrote an article once about the life cycle of Bulletin Boards and Muds, I put forward the theory that people who have been on BBS or the Net for a short time (the boy racers?) are naturally aggressive to the new arrivals because it reminds them that they used to be like that themselves – I guess there's a school mentality about it, the 2nd and 3rd years think they run the school and bully the first years and the 6th formers just keep out of it. Does it really matter to anyone if someone has a signature bigger than 3 lines? What pleasure do you get out of being rude to someone you don't know and ruining their perceptions of this wonderful technology so early on? If they make a mistake, tell them gently, don't shoot them, remember, we are meant to be civilised!

I am not trying to achieve anything, I am not on a mission, I'll leave that to someone else. I will 'win' in the end anyway, because there will just be too many people around for you all to show how streetwise you are to. Your mates may appreciate the fact that your Ford RS Turbo is tuned to perfection, but frankly, I don't think you'll find the family of 6 in the Renault Espace will give a toss.

For now, the roads and the playgrounds are still yours, enjoy them whilst you can – It's not too nice to see a world you once knew change so dramatically........"

© Michael Lawrie '95 – michael@uknet.com – http://www.uknet.com/nasty.com/f-o-d.txt

Of course, things have changed an awful lot since 1995, and much of what Lawrie said has come true.

Are you sure you want to complain?

What may seem so obviously rude to you may just have been an innocent mistake on the part of the poster, and they may not be so well versed in the nuances of online etiquette as you will be by the end of this book.

Being prudish will not win you respect in any quarter, but if someone really has been offensive, then surely it is sensible to ask for an apology before mouthing off to their system administrator to get their account terminated. Really, that doesn't make you any better than them, does it?

Okay, so you do!

If you know the domain from which the user comes, the first course of action is to send a polite mail to the system administrator. Include time-stamped logs of all the offending communiques together with a brief explanation of why you think the user was in error, and what action you would like to be taken.

The e-mails should be addressed to the postmaster mailbox. If you were sending a mail to complain about me you would send one to *postmaster@journalism.demon.co.uk* and another to *postmaster@demon.net*. Every responsible mail administrator should read mail sent to these addresses. In the first case I would receive the mail to the *journalism.demon.co.uk* domain, whilst the latter would go to my ISP, Demon Internet.

ISPs will usually only act against abuse OF the Net, not abuse ON the Net.

If the complaint is regarding a Usenet or e-mail post then, there is often a header generated either by the news server or the client to direct abuse complaints. The newsreader Demon Internet supplies with their starter pack, Turnpike, generates an *X-Abuse: abuse@demon.net* header, so complaints should also be directed to this mailbox.

If you don't get any luck there then try to find the name of the domain registrant. If it is a UK domain then go to *http://www.nominet.org* or if it is a general International domain then go to *http://rs.internic.net* and type in the name of the domain – eg, *netculture.org* in the WHOIS lookup box.

```
Registrant:

   Josh Smith (NETCULTURE4-DOM)
     Computer Step
     Southfield Road, Southam, Warks. CV33 0FB
     UK

     Domain Name: NETCULTURE.ORG

     Administrative Contact, Technical Contact, Zone Contact:
        Nicholson, Jules  (JN874)  jules@JUNIC.NET
        +44 (0)956 321432 (FAX) +44 (0)181 974 9955

     Domain servers in listed order:

     NS1.EASYPOST.COM          207.153.241.133
     NS.UKMAIL.ORG             195.112.37.34
```

Chapter Eight

Online Shopping

In this chapter we discuss the pros, cons and social effects of selling and purchasing on the Internet, together with likely implications for the retailing industry.

Covers

What Does It Offer?

Ever heard the phrase 'shop till you drop'? Although shopping can be a pleasant activity when it involves a small number of presents and the like, speaking from a male bias, trawling through Sainsburys or Tescos isn't exactly my idea of fun.

Of course, the wonders of technology have offered us a solution to this drudgery. The Internet offers a much more convenient option. All you have to do is zap over to the site of the supermarket of your choice, clickety click on the products you want on your list and 'hey presto' – they arrive the next day on your doorstep.

However, although the men (and women) in white coats have offered us a 'solution' to the problem, retailers have been rather slow to take up on it.

Retail resistance

In the UK in particular, the idea of supermarket trolleys free-wheeling down the Infobahn isn't one that major retailers have been quick to embrace. The reasons for this are threefold.

Firstly, large companies are slow to pick up on new technologies – particularly ones which involve a great deal of expense. Although large corporates are quite willing to spend a few hundred thousand pounds on a flashy web presence and smatter it over their carrier bags, they are hesitant to splash out tens of millions on a project in an area which many of them have limited experience – mail order.

Secondly, for the largest of retailers, who can afford this sort of outlay, it isn't going to significantly increase their customer base. There is a Tescos, Sainsburys, Dixons or Wickes in almost every major town and city, and given the relative expense of goods in the UK, it isn't going to help them expand their custom in an international sense.

Lastly, the number of people online compared to the overall populace is still quite small (10%), and for many, the weekly trip to the supermarket is as much a social activity as much as it is a necessity. A place where you meet friends and browse for new products, it has an almost ritualistic place in modern society.

Division of markets

When we consider this topic we need to divide the retail sector into two distinct areas: common / perishable goods, and luxury goods.

The first, being the province of Safeway, Somerfield, Sainsburys and their ilk, has the advantage of being a regular activity, but suffers from a lower price margin and smaller expenditure on bulkier goods. If they are perishable, effective transportation can be costly.

Secondly, mail order has rarely worked in the past as people want to see and feel what they intend to buy, and many consumers actually enjoy navigating their squeaky trolleys between the frozen counter and the fruit 'n' veg – as well as a cup of tea afterwards.

Luxury goods are a much more obvious market for online retailers. Although it is quite possible to envisage Dixons taking the plunge into the electronic 'peddling pool', they would be competing with companies such as Argos, who are much better equipped to deal with mail order supplies.

So why aren't Argos out there, flogging their wares on the Net? Firstly, we have to recognise that the advantage for them is minimal. Most people have a catalog kicking around their house somewhere, and it's just as convenient to flick through that and ring the freephone number than mess about with web sites and online credit verification.

Secondly, given the falling cost of international carriers, Argos might be competing with retailers in Taiwan selling direct from source, and at much lower margins. Most high street chains lose their advantage (their high street presence) online, where they are set to compete against prices they cannot match. The market has to be filled from somewhere else, but where?

How Does It Work?

You can essentially divide online retail outlets into three distinct categories: independent sites, dependent sites and retail malls.

Retail malls

These were the first fully functional shopping outlets on the Internet. At a time when such sites were few and far between, and the technology needed to make them work was relatively expensive, they allowed companies to band together and reduce financial outlay – as well as making them easier to find.

Probably the most famous of these malls was Barclaysquare. This turned out to be something of a flop. The reason for this had a lot to do with problems related to the convenient transference of money. Also, when it was conceived, four years ago, the customer base was much smaller than it is today – and consumer confidence in the technology was lacking.

Independent sites

Credit verification ensures that a credit card is valid and is used by the appropriate person.

Despite the sound philosophy of the original idea, many established retailers became wary of the 'net market' concept. For unestablished retailers, who later came to prominence on the Net, the opportunity to join malls and markets was not available.

So companies such as Amazon and CDNow! set up their own sites and raised sufficient investment to give their ideas a breath of reality – with the falling cost of credit verification and web server setups, as well as a growing online customer base.

Dependent sites

These are a relatively new idea, bridging the gap between the advantages of interlinking that the mall system offered, but without all the inevitable complications of competition.

For example, if you run an information resource for Star Trek fans you could set up a little mini bookshop (aided by Amazon or Bookpages) offering Star Trek titles exclusively.

It would then link to the main site and a percentage of each book sale, typically 10%-20%, would be given to the dependent maintainer.

Credit verification

The public perceive the electronic transmission of credit card details to be insecure, which is strange considering that most people wouldn't hesitate to voice their digits over a telephone line.

First of all you should look for a site which offers a 'secure channel' to stop data being intercepted by uninvited parties. Most serious sites use SSL – a Secure Sockets Layer. Modern browsers tend to support it; Internet Explorer and Navigator certainly do.

Secure is a relative term. SSL makes the channel secure, but it doesn't make the information being transmitted secure – for that an encryption protocol is needed.

The SET (Secure Electronic Transactions) protocol is based on public key cryptography – the same concept as the PGP program discussed in the chapter 'Online Protection'. In a SET transaction, each party is identified by a digital certificate.

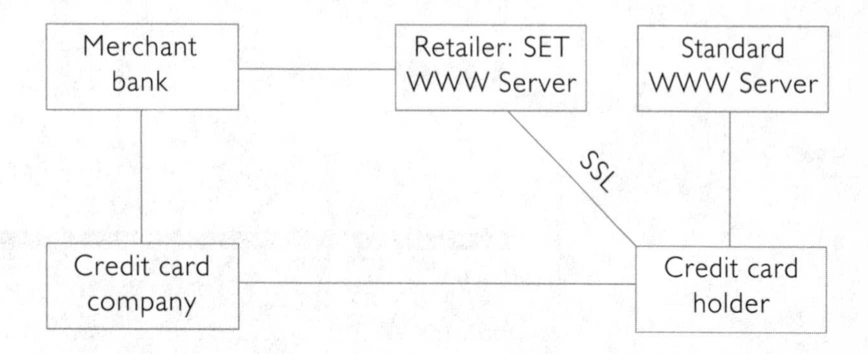

In the verification system the access of each participant is limited. For example, the credit card holder cannot communicate with the systems of the merchant bank, nor can the retailer review the information held by the credit card company on the client in question.

In the exchanges, each participant has at least two public and private pairs of keys. This ensures that security is more likely to be compromised by human ineptness than by technological vulnerabilities. Heavy use of encryption does, however, make the actual exchange of data very slow and resource intensive.

If you don't understand what 'public' and 'private' keys are then read the section on 'privacy and encryption' in Chapter Nine.

For both security and pragmatic reasons a separate server is often used to handle secure transactions, whilst the main server (or the main server 'farm' for substantial sites) feeds the site's content.

Leaving the technical gubbins aside for a moment, it is important that you understand whether a transaction is secure or not. There follows a list of things you should look for:

1. The Security Information Dialog Box.
2. The unbroken padlock or key.

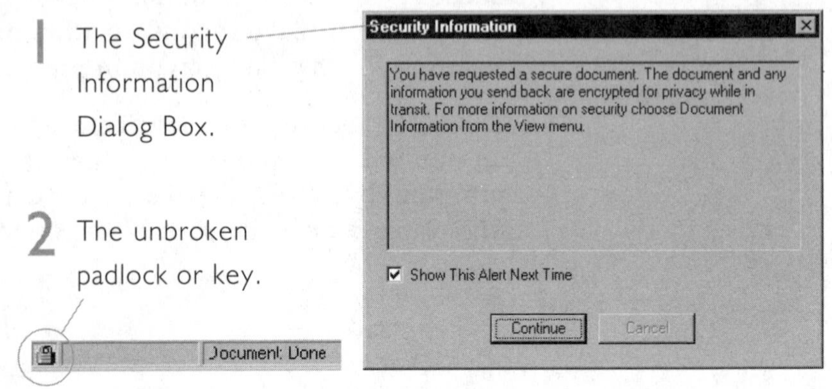

3. 'https://' rather than 'http://'.

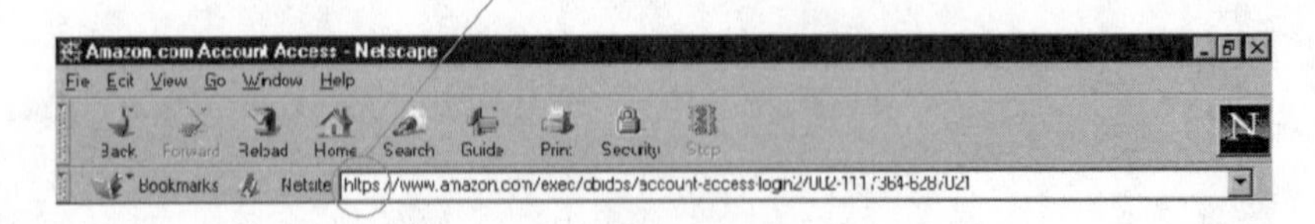

Providing a little bit of caution is exercised, along with some common sense, you should find electronic commerce is a very secure way of conducting business. You may not feel comfortable ordering online now, but the day when everyone is digitising their digits is surely not far away.

Making It Work For You

For the Internet retailer there is a potentially huge customer base to exploit, but the online markets are not easy to navigate – as the largely unsuccessful recent endeavours have shown.

Although the advantages of having an existing corporate presence and brand may *seem* obvious for any company venturing online, it doesn't always confer quite the advantages you expect.

Firstly, unless you own Nike, Coca-Cola or Pepsico, your brand is unlikely to have international appeal. A strong retail chain in America, such as Barnes & Noble, may have no identity in the UK or in Europe as a whole – just in the same way as most people across the pond wouldn't be familiar with Marks & Spencers, Sainsburys or Tescos.

Secondly the Internet consumer has, certainly in the past, been someone who is used to purchasing products which don't have a recognisable brand. Sure, Microsoft might be famous, but the volatility of the software market makes brand loyalty less important.

Numerous web hosts use freeware or shareware software such as Apache, and top their equipment with little known Unix variants or even the open source Linux, in preference to Windows NT. The same is true with hardware. Although Dell, Elonex or Gateway may be reliable brands, consumers primarily look for specifications at cheap prices. Support is obviously a factor, but for the home consumer it has always taken the back burner, as far as desirability goes.

With more and more non-technical people diving into the cyber ether, the typical netizen is converging with the profile of the average member of the general populace, but we sure aren't there yet.

Services

Internet related services are always popular. Hotmail, now owned by Microsoft, offers free e-mail services; Geocities offer free web space – there are even a few companies which offer a free limited dial up / e-mail service of some kind.

The problem with the Internet is the premise on which it is based. You pay for your ISP connection and you pay for your telephone bill, but given the limited commercial presence on the Net in the past, everything else has been offered on an altruistic basis – usually at the expense of Universities and government institutions.

For this reason, netizens weren't willing to pay for e-mail addresses or web space – so companies had to find a different way to create revenue.

Advertising

You will often see banners on search engines, and 'service' sites. Payment based on a click-through rate has become prevalent over a flat fee. Typically this is charged at 2p to 8p per 'impression'. It can cost tens of thousands of pounds to link people to your site in this way, but in commercial terms that is really very little to base revenue upon.

Products

Although service based sites have been moderately successful, sites selling actual products have encountered more resistance. You need to think about the way people use the Internet to think whether they are actually going to buy a product online or not.

Firstly, is the product one which most people would normally entrust to mail order? Okay, flower delivery, CDs, books, ermmm....ermm...

There are many others, but a second point you have to consider is that many people are wary of making large purchases over the Internet. They are worried about security, more due to rumour than recent personal experience.

Thirdly, excessively bulky goods (which cost a lot to transport across large distances) or goods specific to a region or country have limited appeal on the Internet as they have a significantly smaller potential market. This isn't such a problem if Alamo LA wants to run a 'rent-a-car' scheme online, as many tourists will be attracted to it, and California is the 'wired' state – where netizens breed like rabbits, or so they say. If however, you offer a grocery service for the Shetland Isles, then investing heavily on a web presence may not be appropriate.

Pornography

Perhaps the most depressing thing about electronic consumerism is that in the twelve months preceding September 1998, $162 million US dollars (£104 million) was spent by consumers online, of which $98 million (£61 million) was spent on pornographic or sex related, visual and literary material.

There is a difference between online consumerism and electronic commerce. Unfortunately, like most things, they mean something different to everyone. Suffice to say that online consumerism covers products bought with credit cards – and it's what we're really interested in.

The future

E-Commerce businesses and forecasters get awfully excited about the future role of the Internet in the world markets, despite the fact that even some of the most successful of online retailers (Amazon being a good example) have as yet failed to make a profit.

Despite a rather poor understanding in the industry of what electronic commerce actually is, Forrester, Jupiter and IDC all have estimates between $6 billion dollars and $8 billion dollars for gross turnover in the year 2000.

Of course, electronic commerce projections are rather tainted by bias. The CEO of Cisco Systems seems to think that electronic commerce will account for $1.5 trillion dollars of world trade by 2000. Hardly impartial since Cisco are one company which has a lot to gain from a rush to the Web. Of course, it all depends how you define 'e-commerce' – after all, banks exchange money by electronic means as well....but that's another story.

Where To Start...

- *http://www.amazon.com/*

  Rather useful, this one. Amazon is the largest book retail outlet on the Net, and its prices considerably undercut those of most UK bookshops. They also sell CDs and sheet music, amongst other products. Well worth a visit.

- *http://www.computerstep.com*

  Much closer to home is the site for the publishers of this book. Books can be purchased directly through a secured server. Post and packaging is less, and books are priced in pounds sterling, which makes things simpler.

- *http://www.cdnow.com/*

  A rather fab online music store, with a much larger range of audio material than Amazon's selection. Clips are also available, although they require specific plugins, which is a bit of a pain.

- *http://www.barclaysquare.com/*

  After a recent overhaul, the Barclaysquare site has improved a great deal. Certainly worth looking at, with lots of shops, although most are mere external links – rather than actually being local to the Barclaysquare site. Definitely deserves a quick peek.

Chapter Nine

Online Protection

In this chapter, we look at how to protect yourself and your computer from miscreants on the Internet. We also look at where you can find data stored about you online, and how you can keep the most secret of information private from prying eyes.

Covers

Privacy and Encryption

For information on credit card security and the electronic transmission of private details, see Chapter Eight.

It's secret, it's private, it's personal – and you don't want everyone to know about it. The Internet may be a complex system of information dispersal, but sometimes there is some information you just don't want dispersed.

The first electronic computer, Colossus, was built during the Second World War to crack the German Enigma codes. 50 years on, cryptography is still an important technological craft.

Although in times past encryption was generally only of interest to paranoid nerds, the military and large companies, the ability of the Internet to communicate undesirable information makes keeping such information secure more important than ever.

Conventional Cryptography

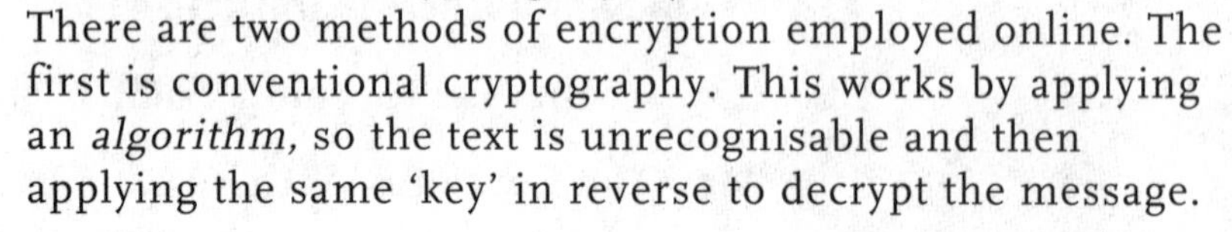

There are two methods of encryption employed online. The first is conventional cryptography. This works by applying an *algorithm,* so the text is unrecognisable and then applying the same 'key' in reverse to decrypt the message.

An algorithm, in cryptography terms at least, is a set of instructions which determine how the text is changed to an encrypted form.

A very simple encryption key is ROT-13. This was first used in Roman times by legates to communicate information securely. It isn't very secure, but it is very easy to understand. Sometimes you might see it employed on Usenet to hide obscene or potentially distressing material. Most Usenet clients have the ability to quickly rotate and unrotate ROT-13 material.

If we took a short string of text such as this:

Doner kebabs and lager don't mix

The 'ciphertext' or the encrypted message, using ROT-13 would look something like this:

Qbare xronof naq yntre qba'g zvk

Great, huh? Completely secure and indecipherable to prying eyes. Well no, not really. What the key actually does is rotate each letter 13 characters round the alphabet, so in practise it isn't going to take long to crack.

'Public-Key' cryptography

The problem with single key systems is that the message is only as secure as the channel upon which the key is transmitted. Two-key systems work differently.

You have two keys: a public key and a secret (or private) key. Anyone can encrypt a message using a public key, but the message can only be decrypted using the secret key from which the public key is derived.

This is more convenient since you don't have to have a separate key for each of your 'sinister' friends. Also, the public key is readily available so you can receive private messages, even from people who you wouldn't necessarily expect to receive such information from.

The name PGP (Pretty Good Privacy) may not inspire confidence, but it is the premier form of encryption technology. Created by Phil Zimmermann, it is based upon the RSA public key systems and is, to date, virtually impossible to break.

The US government threw an absolute fit when they heard about PGP. It's a very long story, but PGP is freely available and free in monetary terms as well. It is however a 'munition' and thus only a weaker, 'international' version is legally available to people outside the US – a bit pathetic, since the real McCoy is still easy to get hold of, no matter where you are.

'To err is human'

The real problem with modern encryption isn't the technology itself, but the way in which it is used – ie, in appropriate or inappropriate circumstances.

The first problem works on what is called the 'sore thumb' theory:

The sore thumb theory: If we cast our eyes backwards, technologically speaking, to look at the traditional system of postal delivery, the analogies regarding security are rather apparent.

If you want to send something valuable through the post, like a piece of artwork for example, it is immediately apparent to any would-be criminal what packages to search for such valuable commodities. The one which is about 5 feet long and 2 feet wide is probably a good bet: it sticks out like a sore thumb.

In electronic terms then, the problem is that 99% of all e-mails aren't encrypted, so anyone who intercepts your mail (which isn't difficult) will know which mail has all the valuable gubbins in it.

Going Public: The second problem is one which isn't immediately apparent with two key cryptography, but is the most serious. Take three characters for example. Nephew A wants you (Aunt Amy) to mail him your secret cake recipe. But evil Cousin B wants to steal it and sell it to Mr Kipling.

Nephew A agrees to send you his public key. Cousin B sends you a public key he has created and sends it as though it is from Nephew A. You encrypt the cake recipe with the key, send it back to Cousin B and Nephew A intercepts it. So much for 'strong' encryption.

Now there are ways you can avoid this, such as reading out the key's 'fingerprint' over the phone, but the initial security of the channel is still an issue.

It is rather tempting to get very paranoid on the Internet and encrypt everything, but the simple fact is that unless you are a celebrity, politician or employed by a military intelligence agency, most people don't care sufficiently about what you think to go snooping through your e-mail. Useful to know though!

Big Brother is Watching You...?

The Internet can appear to offer anonymity through the sheer number of people who use it. People will say things to, hear things from, lie to and perhaps most importantly confide things to relative strangers – things which they would not in a million years consider doing in real life.

How you get unstuck..

The problem is that people make the same assumptions on the Net that they make in real life. You talk to someone on IRC who you have never met before. They ask about your marital arrangements. You say you're single, but you're actually married. Could you walk up the high street in a local town, lie blatantly, and without a wedding ring, easily get away with it? We all know the Internet makes lying 'sooooo' easy: you could be eighty-two, and pretend to be twenty-two so how could they find out?

Knowledge is power

It is surprising, sometimes painfully so, how much people can find out. When you registered your IRC client did you fill in the box saying 'e-mail' address? Did you know that by using the 'Finger' command on a user you can obtain their e-mail address?

Now, providing someone has been using an e-mail address for some time, you can find out an incredible amount of information about them, particularly if they are active users.

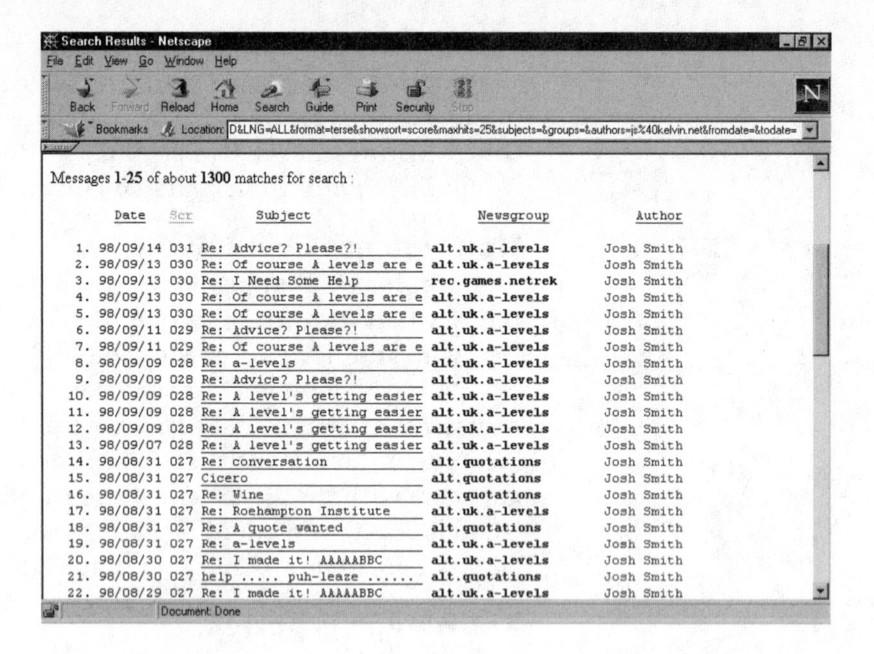

Dejanews

This is probably the most popular news archive tool, and certainly one of the most comprehensive, with its records going back to before 1993. By clicking on 'Power Search' and entering his e-mail address in the 'Author' box you can usually get a whole past history of the person's Usenet activities. You can discuss with them the 'interesting' post they made to *alt.sex.chichua* ... or worse!

On a more sober note, you can find out what they are interested in, who they know and, if you are paranoid, you can correlate what they tell you about themselves with what they say in their posts.

- Available from: *http://www.dejanews.com/*

'/whois'

If you want to obtain some basic information about someone, the first thing you do is employ the 'whois' command. You do this by clicking on your IRC client's 'status' window and typing '/whois'. You should get a response which looks something like this:

```
Josh is js@journalism.demon.co.uk * Josh Smith
Josh using London.UK.EU.Kewl.Org [195.8.71.10] Bogus.Kewl.Org
Josh has been idle 3 seconds, signed on Sun Aug 09 04:55:12
End of /WHOIS list.
-
```

The '/whois' above tells you that my *ident* (a handle which tells the network where I'm coming from) is '*js@journalism.demon.co.uk*', my name is 'Josh Smith'. Other data below includes what server I'm using (which may indicate where in the world I am, if my ident does not – see Chapter Four, country code list), what time I logged on, and how long it is since I typed anything to the server.

How to find me

Assuming a) you don't know my e-mail address and b) you don't know my web site address you can probably ascertain both, either, or one from the other, from the information above.

My web site is undeniably the most useful source of information for any wannabe know-it-all. It is of course relying on the premise that I have one, which isn't consistently true. In my case it's quite easy since Demon Internet (my internet service provider) use fixed IPs.

That means I have an IP (a number that identifies me to the network) and a hostname that is unique to *me,* rather than the modem I'm dialling into. RIPE, who issue the darn things, are running a bit short of them, so newer service providers might only get a few hundred rather than tens of thousands. If my ISP were amongst the newer service providers who have to limit the number they can give out, then you wouldn't know what my host name was without my e-mail address or a successful search on the web.

Ignoring the bit of the ident before the '@' sign (which is useless for our purposes) we could try slapping it into our web browser and waggling it, in numerous different modulations at hypothetical web site addresses.

First of all you could try, *http://journalism.demon.co.uk,* which incidentally doesn't work. One idea is to insert a *'www'.* before the rest of my address. Lo and behold, *'http://www.journalism.demon.co.uk',* so you know everything about me, and conclude of course, what a righteous and honest person I am – either that or I'm a consistent liar.

Let's pretend ...

If that didn't work or didn't help then you can try other things. In the former case there are other permutations you can try. Some service providers have their home pages in a sub directory – for example, *http://www.well.com/joshs/.* It can, however, be more complicated. Some users might have home page directories which are prefixed by a tilde (~) – it's supposed to make your e-mail address look less attractive and amateurish, enticing you to purchase commercial web space, as well as being a Unix convention. In this case my web site address would be *http://www.well.com/~joshs/.*

To a similar effect (these being *real* cases) web hosts often insert the word 'user' or 'members' into the pot. So my site could be at *http://member.xoom.com/joshsmith/* or *http://users.zetnet.co.uk/josh/* or more obscure still *http://dspace.pipex.com/js./*

If you keep plugging away, you're bound to dig up something. However, if all else fails you can try search engines.

Search engines (chug chuga chuga chuga ... weeep)

Leaving aside the infantile train noises, 'finding people out' will often come down to this. There are plenty of web search engines out there, all of which use different search databases so they should come up with different results. The following search has been conducted using Lycos, one of the more popular and venerably old (by search engine standards anyway) databases – plus it's easy to figure out.

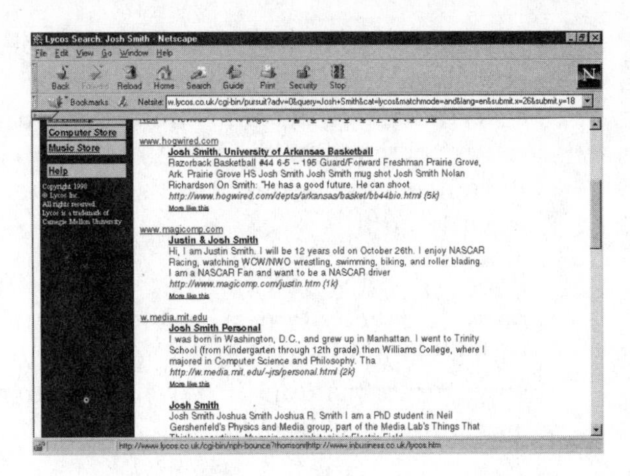

As you can see this method reveals the largest multitude and the most completely and utterly useless results possible. Things do turn up, however.

According to this I could be a basketball player in Arkansas (gosh, and I thought only girls played netball!), or Josh Smith who hosts a particularly weird site called 'the Realm' or even a PhD student at the Massachusetts Institute of Technology, reading Physics. Let me assure you, I am none of the above.

One way to refine the search is to add geographic details, or try sites or engines which deal with specific localities (the *co.uk* in my ident tells you I live or have an Internet presence in the UK). Here are a few good search engines to try:

- *http://www.yahoo.com/, http://www.yahoo.co.uk/*
  Yahoo – the biggest and arguably the best as well.
- *http://www.excite.com/*
  Excite – a popular and comprehensive site.
- *http://www.altavista.com/*
  Altavista – extremely popular and linked to Yahoo, but seems to lack its coherent topic structuring.
- *http://www.lycos.com/*
  Lycos – good for people and places. Plenty of UK stuff.
- *http://www.infoseek.com/*
  Infoseek – another one to try.
- *http://www.hotbot.com/*
  Hotbot – newish, but getting bigger all the time.

May The Force Be With You...

Just in the same way as it is easy to become engrossed in one particular area of the Internet, to the extent that everything else becomes unimportant, it is easy to identify either the good *or* the bad things which this Information Revolution has brought with it, but rather more difficult to identify both.

Personally, I would say that the benefits of the Internet far outweigh the potential problems, but these are problems which should be tackled. They have to be tackled in an appropriate fashion, however – not to the detriment of everything else.

People at the top

The problem is that many of the influential people in both the UK and abroad have only a very limited understanding of what the Internet offers, and the damage which can be caused by overly strict regulation.

Nor do they realise how difficult such legislature is to enforce, given the Net's international dimension. Anything which helps people communicate in an interesting, different and effective new way is undeniably a good thing.

Sure, there is pornography and illegal activity online, but the Internet is merely another vehicle for the conveyance of such material. In essence, the problem is not the Internet, but a small group of the people who use it – so don't shoot the messenger!

Chapter Ten

The Darker Side of the Net

In this chapter we look at a wide assortment of online misdemeanours and contentious issues, attempting to separate the facts from the fiction.

Covers

Internet Law

There is no 'law' on the Internet as such. There are 'guidelines', 'expectations' and the individual legislature of countries where information is stored and exchanged, but there is no universal enforcement of principles. This is because, as we discussed on page 31, no individual person or organisation owns (or controls the owners of) a significant chunk of the 'cyber-ether' (with the possible exception of the US government). There also exists a strong 'anti-control' lobby formed with the influential founding generation of 'public-access' Internet users.

Ownership or regulation of the Internet is limited.

In the face of this, then, enforcing laws *within* the Internet (ie, stopping users doing certain things) is impractical. Alternatively, enforcing laws *against* the Internet – even banning it altogether – is possible, but an extreme measure.

Few governments want to go to the extremes of snipping all the phone lines in their country or leaving their economy dragging behind in the race for online presence, but they would quite like to rid themselves of online fraud, porn, etc. The fact is, you either take it all, or you don't take it at all.

Why does it work?

It may seem strange that an information system, which intrinsically requires structure, works in an environment which is chaotic and unregulated. Fortunately though, users tend to work towards the benefit of the Internet, because an Internet that doesn't work isn't any use or any fun.

Conflicting interests are sometimes a problem. For example, a 'spammer' seeks to make money from the Internet by sending commercial e-mail to everyone, but the majority of the people find his actions ethically objectionable, and therefore socially unacceptable. As a result the spammer becomes a social outcast.

Although the consequences of spamming on the Internet – social alienation for one – are much less than those of, say, corporate fraud, so are the gains. Self-regulation, then, is a much 'healthier' form of control as people don't follow 'the law' because of the fear of reprisal, but because of mutual self-interest.

Phreaking and Hacking

Phreaking is when you mess about with the telephone network, whilst hacking is when you mess about with someone else's computer.

Hollywood, together with the aid of its trusty sidekick, the popular press, has ensured that you are more misinformed about this particular sphere of the Internet than anything else.

You see these films (not mentioning any names here) with spotty 14 year olds sitting at keyboards breaking into banks, police files and school records. Such films make it rather hard to appreciate, nowadays at least, how difficult that is to do.

That's not to say it is impossible to do, especially after a Russian's recent foray into Citibank's electronic treasure chest, but just because your little brother has got a computer, a phone line and an electronic box of tricks connected to both, doesn't mean he'll be able to improve your exam marks or overturn your parking fine. Bad luck.

All things in moderation

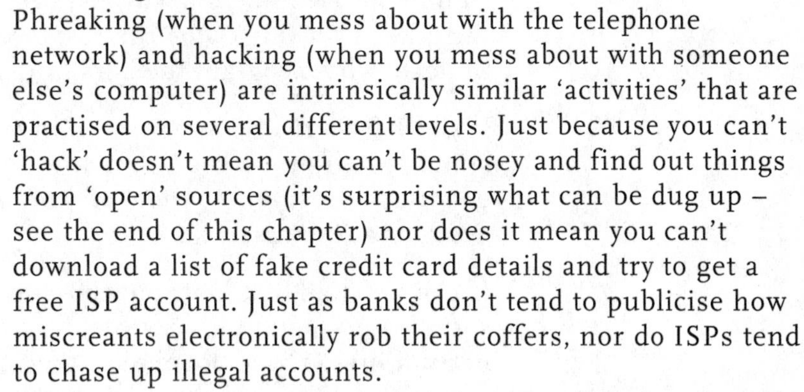

Phreaking (when you mess about with the telephone network) and hacking (when you mess about with someone else's computer) are intrinsically similar 'activities' that are practised on several different levels. Just because you can't 'hack' doesn't mean you can't be nosey and find out things from 'open' sources (it's surprising what can be dug up – see the end of this chapter) nor does it mean you can't download a list of fake credit card details and try to get a free ISP account. Just as banks don't tend to publicise how miscreants electronically rob their coffers, nor do ISPs tend to chase up illegal accounts.

'Hacking' is a bit of a misnomer. A 'hacker' was originally a programmer who could knock together a program very quickly. Unfortunately the term has been popularised and demonised by the national press.

Hiding your tracks in the case of phreaking requires several doctorates in network theory (or just a tremendous affinity to computers and network manuals), and the chances are you'll probably never ever meet anyone on the Internet who possesses the skill to either manage to 'do it' or 'get away with it'. They are a select, and fortunately dying breed.

In the case of hacking, hiding your tracks requires a modicum of understanding, but it's the hacking equivalent of dangling a 10p coin into an old public telephone: it doesn't offer great rewards and it doesn't work very often.

How can I do it?

If I knew how to do it, do you think I would be writing this book? Quite. What you can do, though, is appear vaguely 'clued up' about it.

Being apparently able to 'hack' will make certain sections of the Internet community treat you with great reverence. After all, power and control is something which may be resisted, but that doesn't mean users don't 'admire' it.

Common types of computer misuse

You can flood users with 'requests', which is when you send a piece of information which requires a response. When we talked about networking in Chapter Four, we discussed a *(ctcp) ping* command which exchanged timestamps so you could work out the 'delay' between yourself and another user. This is one example of a 'ctcp' command. Another, such as *ctcp time,* would tell you what the other user thinks the time is, or *ctcp version* would indicate what program the person is using.

If you have a really fast connection you can get a 'bot' (a simple program) to send so many ctcp requests that the client can't respond to them all and the user's machine overloads and 'crashes'.

If you get hold of a 'port pusher' you can exploit bugs in software or operating systems to cause computers to do nasty things. These 'loopholes' tend to be much more frequent under newer operating systems such as Windows than they are under the simpler and more ancient varieties of UNIX.

It makes sense when you consider that people have been trying to break into UNIX based systems for over 30 years, whereas Windows has only been around for half a dozen or so years.

Preventative measures

You would be well advised to get hold of 'patches' (they prevent unsavoury characters taking advantage of product-bugs) to stop yourself being the unfortunate victim of 'nuking' and 'port pushing'. They are regularly available from the web sites of most major IRC networks.

You could also use a firewall, which 'fields' all data accepted and requested and decides what to allow and disallow. Conseal Firewall is quite good for individual users. It's 'shareware' (you pay to use the software after a trial period). If you go to the additional length of watching the 'port scanner' you can see who is trying to mess about with your PC. Great, huh?

Hacking culture

A good way to obtain a bit of aforementioned 'hacking clue' is to have a read of some e-zines (electronic magazines) which are freely available on the Web.

'Phreak' is a newsletter which has been going for yonks and yonks, and is interesting in a vague sort of way, but technophobes beware, it can get a bit complicated. Originally it only covered telephone related crime, but now it concerns itself with the whole caboodle.

The 2600 project was originally an (illegal) idea for obtaining calls to anywhere in the world at local call rate. It worked, and not surprisingly proved quite popular – especially when you consider most Internet users' phone bills.

The theory was that you sounded a 2600hz tone (it was actually 2280hz in the UK) down the phone, you could chitter chatter to your friend in Nairobi or New York as cheaply, as you could to someone in say, Newcastle. As a point of interest, before the various telecommunications companies changed their exchanges, Captain Crunch (in the US) gave away free whistles in their cereal packets and it just so happened that these produced a tone of 2600hz. Fortified with added value, if only Snap, Crackle and Pop could do the same?

Illegal Software Online

It is important to remember that a great deal of the software available online, particularly that which is overtly advertised, is not illegal. Sometimes it may be shareware, to entice users to buy a fully featured and more expensive version. More often than not it is given away free by some net-based kindred spirit, or, in the case of Internet browsers, by a huge multi-national trying to gain a larger market share.

Warez

Pronounced 'Wares' (it's that cool spelling again!) this is a generic term for copied software, and includes cracks (software that's been disassembled to remove security features or more usually serial numbers) and 'hacks' (the same thing usually).

It's available from numerous sources. The *alt.binaries. warez* hierarchies on Usenet are absolutely full of the stuff, but there is no guarantee that it has all the bits with it, or, worse, that it even works at all. There are also web sites which carry material, but they don't tend to last long, particularly if they are on free storage offered by companies such as Xoom and Geocities. Beware of geeks bearing false GIFs (pronounced 'giffs').

The way that this problem tends to be circumvented is that the sites are advertised on IRC channels. The pages themselves are often filled out with porn advertising banners (the page maintainers get a few cents per click) to allow their designers to profit from their online 'business' ventures.

Why isn't illegal software readily available?

A rather obvious reason for this is that it's illegal, and it's difficult for people to make money from it. Unless they have a crusade against capitalism, or a love for heavy fines and prison bars, they tend not to do it.

Secondly, and rather less obviously, a program such as PageMaker (used to write this book) is 60mb (zipped up) which twenty or thirty times over is a considerable amount of disk space, but also puts a considerable strain on a web site host's ISP connection. A few people downloading a few big files can saturate a connection for several hours.

Thirdly, and finally, it is painfully slow for the recipient if they are retrieving it across a normal phone line or a server which is quite remote from them. At most they aren't going to get more than 6kb/a sec (it would take you about four hours to download Quake), which, with blips and disconnects, means you have to sit and monitor it. Watching paint dry? Yeah, right!

Downloading illegal software from the Internet is time consuming and frustrating – it's not worth bothering!

All of which means it's probably cheaper, quicker and easier to copy it off a friend, a work colleague, the next door neighbour or a second cousin twice removed – you get the gist?

A bad deal then?

Well, that depends! FAST (the Federation Against Software Theft) would love to get their hands on you, although generally software companies are only interested in apprehending dealers and distributors. Every visit you make to a web site is traceable, as you leave digital footprints – an IP address – in your wake.

To conclude, downloading illegal software is time consuming and tedious and of course it's wrong, but then it is a lot cheaper if it works. Many software firms actually profit from people using illegal programs, because many users eventually register the application or purchase it for the companies they work for. The real problem isn't legality, but practicality, and that isn't going to change any time soon.

Pornography

To a much greater extent than illegal software, pornography on the Internet is rife. You can't sit in an IRC channel without being bombarded with 'see my sex site' messages (they are automated clients, by the way) or your mail box exploding with 'XXX visit here' junk post. Indeed, porn sites seem to have a semi-monopoly on UCE (Unsolicited Commercial E-mail) – everything else runs a poor second.

This isn't surprising, because the porn business is big business, accounting for thousands of millions of dollars online. In fact it makes more money than the rest of the electronic commerce sector put together. When Bill Gates wrote about 'The Road Ahead' I doubt he thought the sensual 'superhighway' would end up in a brothel.

Legality

That's the way it is, for better or for worse. The actual legality of the sites is questionable: not because of their content (which, depending on where they are located, may or may not be unlawful) but that most of the pictures or stories have been stolen from other sites and are thus in breach of copyright.

Internet Relay Chat

Alternative sources for free material to satiate your sexual desires are available, just not so obvious. 'FSERVE' bots on IRC offer material for download, although they can be a little bit difficult to navigate.

The instant accessibility and limbo-like state of IRC (although hosts might pull the plug on a web site, they would rarely detect a malevolent IRC client) also makes it ideal for distributing site passwords which can get you into the aforementioned 'pay-for' sites.

There are some private collections available. They tend to contain text-based material rather than pictures, since the strain on the web host is substantial enough to make finding one with large enough connections a very difficult or very expensive task.

Usenet binaries

Despite being an unsuitable network for the distribution of binary files such as pictures, commercial porn hosts often post free samples to the erotica newsgroups with the aim of attracting users to their site.

The newsagent theory

This is one idea that is frequently touched upon by writers *about* pornography rather than writers *of* pornography. The argument is that pornography on the Internet isn't any more difficult to find, or any worse than what you might find, on the top shelf of a newsagent's rack. Well, I would suppose that the former is true, and really nasty stuff (paedophilia, bestiality, S&M and the like) is much harder to dig up.

What it does allow is people who wouldn't normally walk up to the counter and actually pay for a porn mag to hide behind a flickery PC monitor and purloin at will. The question really is one of individual morality, with the Internet merely creating increased availability. The Net doesn't create the 'problem' (if you consider it to be a problem) although it does exacerbate it.

Spam

Welcome to *Tinned Meat in easy steps,* a book desig..... ermmm wrong manuscript perhaps? You should feel glad that I saved you from the excessively lame puns and corny cracks which tend to popularise this topic.

The jokes may be contrived, but the problem is not. With it making up almost 40% of Usenet traffic and hitting millions of mailboxes each day, spam is a growing problem, and one that is here to stay.

'Spam', as the generic term, fits into several well-defined groups: unsolicited commercial e-mail, mass-messaging and 'velveeta' (or Usenet spam as it more commonly referred to).

Ad-mail

As far as 'types' of Spam go, they also fit into several pocket-sized categories. The most common type is ad-mail or XXX-mail, the vast majority of which are for porn sites advertising their web presence.

They aren't particularly original or ingenious marketing ploys as the example below illustrates, although some do go as far as making up their own Senate bills.

Don't ever send the remove command to the spammer: their address ends up on a list of '30 million genuine e-mail addresses' and gets even more.

THE LATEST IN ADULT TECHNOLOGY!!!
BRAND NEW XXX ADULT SITE
FREE TRIAL MEMBERSHIP

Please visit the latest in Live Video Conferencing.
1000 channels of hardcore!! Live rooms!!! Young dancers!!!

This message is sent in compliance of
the new e-mail bill:SECTION 301*

* "Per Section 301, Paragraph (a)(2)(C) of S. 1618, further transmissions to you by the sender of this e-mail may be stopped at no cost to you by sending a reply to this e-mail address with the word "remove" in the subject line."

Make Money Fast

Other variants include MMF (Make Money Fast) or MLM (Multi-level Marketing – known to everyone else as Many Losing Money) mails which offer a quick remedy to all your financial problems. Pyramid posts and chain mail fits into this group, which look something like this:

> Hopefully my name is still on the list below. I am a retired attorney, and about two years ago a man came to me with a letter. The letter he brought me is basically the same as the letter in front of you now. When I first read the letter I thought it was some off-the-wall idea to make money. A week later I met again with my client to discuss the issue. I told him that the letter originally brought to me was not 100% legal. My client asked me to alter the letter to make it 100% legal. I advised him to make a small change in the letter and it would be alright.
>
> I was curious about the letter, so he told me how it works. I thought it was a long shot, so I decided against participating. Before my client left, I asked him to keep me updated as to his results. About two months later he called to tell me that he had received over $800,000 in cash!
>
> I was earning a good living as a lawyer, but as anyone in the legal profession will tell you, there is a lot of stress that comes with the job. I told myself if things worked out I would retire from practice and play golf. I sent out 500 letters. Well, three months later I had totaled $2,344,178.00!!! I just couldn't believe it. This is what you have to do.
>
> A) Immediately send $1.00 to each of the six people on the list below.
>
> 1) Success Communication PO Box 721154 Berkley, MI 48072
> 2) Marty Centala 79 N. Trumbull Rd. Bay City, MI 48708
> 3) Michelle Drysdale 2511 – 13th St. Columbus, IN 47201
> 4) Shimshock 121 Harbor Way Ann Arbor, MI 48103
> 5) MT Orsburn, 615 Gardenview Circle, Denton Tx. 76207
> 6) Mohammed Sharief Ali, P.O.Box 7905, Dubai, United Arab Emirates.
>
> Remove the name next to #1 on the list and move the rest of the names up one position. Then place your name in the #6 spot. This is best done by typing a new list and taping or gluing it over the old one.
>
> All you have to do is cut and paste e-mail Addresses wherever you are on the Internet. Remember, it doesn't cost anything to mail on the Internet.

There are three things to remember from this post. Firstly, that chain letter scams don't work; secondly that e-mail costs money to both send and, more importantly, *receive;* and thirdly that you should never trust a lawyer on a golf course.

Munging

One way to stop yourself being the next victim of bulk e-mail is to munge your e-mail address. Take, for example, my address, *js@computerstep.com*. I might change my reply address to *js@spamblock.computerstep.com*. Most users would know to remove the *'spamblock'* from the address, but many automated e-mail robots do not.

Killfiling

Another technique to avoid Spam is to configure your newsreader and e-mail to filter out messages which come from certain addresses.

So if you set it to ignore all postings from *cyberpromo.com*, a notorious e-mail posting and harvesting company, run by the infamous Sanford Wallace, and from *xxx.com*, one of the porn merchant's minions, then you might reduce your share of unsolicited mail. Usually you will simply ignore the post, or if you are using SMTP to retrieve your mail, it will bounce it back to the sender of the offending material. If they send out a thousand mails and three thousand bounce back it can really wind them up.

Even if you use one of the Advertisers' blacklists readily supplied across the Net, you are unlikely to catch more than half of the malevolent messages.

One solution is to ignore all posts which contain a specified text string in their subject line and/or message body. For example, *'xxx'*, *'sex'* or *'jpg'* (the file type which porn pics are usually propagated in).

Either way, you aren't going to get rid of all the trash, and the time you invest in trying to avoid it could probably be better spent ignoring it. Damn shame.

Chapter Eleven

Memoirs of a Byte Gobbling Nerd

It could be said that this is the section for all the stuff that doesn't fit in anywhere else, except of course that would make me appear completely inept. Suffice to say that if you are someone who has never used the Internet before, this is a chapter that will answer some of the questions you have yet to ask.

Covers

Why Do People Use The Internet?

A big question. Let's start with an easier one. Why do I use the Internet? Well, obviously I use it for work – e-mail and web research are essential to what I do. I use it for recreation, and IRCing (which also helps me build up networks of contacts – or so I kid myself when the BT bill arrives).

Everyone is different

That's the point you see, not everyone will have the same perspective on the 'most important thing' that the Internet can do. When a business executive only uses e-mail and the web, it is understandable that he or she may think that not only are these the most useful elements, but even worse, the only elements. The typical response: 'IRC, Usenet – yeah I read about it in a book once. Nerdy stuff. I don't do nerdy stuff.'

In the same way, many Usenetters don't use IRC, many people on IRC don't use Usenet – most of these people use the Web and e-mail, but many wouldn't consider it that important.

Aye, the Net is all a question of perspective, and don't think writers of Net Culture books are any more omniscient than anyone else. If you read John Seabrook's highly acclaimed book 'Deeper', you would find that a third of the book talks about his e-mails with Bill Gates, another third about the WELL and various bits of everything else gets condensed into the last third.

Yet, if he considers the WELL to be such an important part of the online landscape, why has it only garnered a page in my book? The reason, is first of all, that this is primarily a book for UK readers, whereas the WELL is a primarily American forum. But that doesn't really explain why I've given it so little attention.

You see, from my perspective, the WELL is just an overgrown bulletin board, which happens to have some rather influential people on it. The fact you have to pay an additional $10 a month to use it rather grates on my idealistic, 'free net' ideals.

The fact is that the Internet is a BIG place, and in much the same way that you can't see all of Disneyland in a day, you can't see all of the Internet in a lifetime – every time you go back it has changed!

What kind of people use the Internet?

This question is much more difficult to answer than it would have been ten years ago. Nowadays, a huge variety of people use the Internet, and there is a vast array of things which attract people's attention.

For example, the typical character profile of a WELL user is very different from that of someone who uses MUDs or talks in mysteriously hidden IRC channels.

You would find that almost every IRC user has a bit of nerd within themselves, whilst most Usenet posters have a bit of Martin Luther King's egalitarian attitudes at heart.

Do people make the Net, or the Net the people?

Cryptic. It would seem to me that the former is certainly more prevalent than the latter. Usenet is a mine of useless information, because Usenetters in general have a great love for trivia (one that isn't common in the populace as a whole).

On a more morose note, IRCers can be bad communicators in real life, so IRC is stereotyped as a communications medium for people who have no 'real friends'.

The effect is cumulative. If a medium is honed in a particular direction by those who use it, it is therefore likely that it will continue to attract similar types of people to those who already use it.

Of course, the newsgroup *alt.writing* doesn't just attract writers but writer wannabe's, and Usenet doesn't just attract people who are skilled debaters, but incessant arguers as well. The flip side of the coin is that the various facets of the Net tend to only effect the type of users they draw towards themselves, rather than the quality of participation – because, the Internet is a nonexclusive medium.

IRC To RL: Meeting People

Meeting people in real life who you have previously only known through the tippety tapping of a coffee stained keyboard is a rather peculiar experience. Stranger still, it gets more peculiar the better you know them online.

The first thing to realise is that everyone is different – I spent the last two pages ranting about this, but realise that this is very, very important, and so there are no hard and fast rules about what to expect.

How people meet....

Many channels have group meets, where they go to a pub or a restaurant, which are often quite good and well worth attending. Obviously the more internationally diverse a channel is, the harder they are to organise.

In some ways this can be a good thing, and in some ways it can be a bit bad. It's much more fun meeting people in real life that you know on IRC really well. If you don't know most of the people in a channel that well, you can get rather disenchanted with the idea of channel meets.

The advantage of them is that if you don't like a particular person, or you find them shockingly different to what you expected you can always slip away and talk to someone else. Harsh, cruel, but indeed true.

Meeting someone on their own

This is probably the most scary proposition of all, because although you know them really well in some respects, in others you know very little about them at all.

Of course, lurking at the back of your mind is the feeling that what they say in the papers just might be true – particularly if you are a woman.

What if he's a serial rapist, or a mass murderer or...the list goes on. It could perhaps be argued that the Internet *does* attract socially repressed people, and that a small minority of these people may feel so frustrated that they lose their concern for the well-being of others. However, the chances of this are remote.

Being sensible, being cautious

There is no harm in being a little wary. Meet whoever it is you are going to see in a public place – not at their home – and don't be too definite about your plans or arrangements for the rest of day. If you get the measure of the person, and decide they don't quite size up, it will give you a good opt-out clause for rushing off and doing something else.

If you feel uncomfortable say so, and also remember that this isn't a stranger you are talking to: in fact it's someone you know really quite well (although that may be difficult to relate to the physical presence you see before you). Tell them how you feel; talk to them in the same way as you do on IRC. They clearly like you, else they wouldn't have wanted to meet you – so be yourself!

Avoiding unexpected contact

If you are scared, paranoid, or both, be careful about where you put information about yourself – don't be too specific about where you live and don't give out phone numbers or addresses, as one can be determined from the other.

Be sensible and be cautious when you meet people from the Net in real life – but most of all, be yourself.

If people do regularly ask for your home address, consider getting a PO Box mail account, which are relatively cheap. If you want to speak to people, give them your mobile phone number, if you have one. When phoning people, you can dial '141' first which will hide your telephone number from caller id machines.

Most of all, don't be pressured into things online, if you don't like what they are saying, tell them. If they are being annoying then just close the window and ignore them. They're only words after all.

The final word

In essence, don't be discouraged, even if the person you meet isn't quite the person you expect. It is a thoroughly interesting experience – you'll never think about people online in the same way again. It makes the very unreal world of the Net seem very, very real.

The Media and the Internet

Generally speaking, the media doesn't warm to the Internet, and to outsiders it's sometimes difficult to understand why. I remember writing an article for one of the National newspapers, and when phoning them up was shouted at by a particularly stressed, exceptionally unfriendly news room editor: 'bleh, you use way too many technical terms. Internet, software – what are they?' This is the same breed of editor who still used a typewriter until he had one of those snazzy new terminals fitted into his office, which to this day he probably doesn't like, want or trust.

Many other books have expressed the opinion that the media doesn't like the Internet because it sees it as a threat to conventional journalism. This may be true to an extent, but remember that most of the hard nuts who sit at the editorial desk think that it's all just a fad, some kind of technological ogre that will disappear eventually – it won't!

Specialist magazines

These are much more informative regarding Internet related issues than the mainstream press. Some of their content can be a little bit tiresome, where it seems like they regurgitate the same tutorial on 'how to connect to your ISP' every month. I think they could do with more opinion columns personally: *'.net'* has a very groovy writing style, while *'Internet Magazine'* is a bit more sensible, but well written (hey, I'm fishing for good reviews here) – but you should treat the ISP ratings with caution.

Online e-zines

These are getting bigger, but most of all they're getting sponsored as well – therefore, the writers get paid decent amounts of money. As a source of technology related news, *http://www.wired.com/* is just the best, but better still it's free. The site does look a bit tacky, but the content is excellent and covers several stories a day.

The Web will threaten the position of the traditional paper and ink press, but both are here to stay – at least until they invent an e-zine you can read in the bath.

Explaining the Net to your Mum

I am making some rather stereotypical generalisations here. For all I know your Mum may have a degree in Information Science and use the Internet with such skill and dexterity that she embarrasses you at every turn.

In the likely event that this is not the case, I can't really offer any hard and fast solutions to this dilemma. They will undoubtedly be interested, as mothers always are, but a suitable answer can be elusive.

Mum: What do you do with it?

Son: Lots of things.

Mum: What kind of things?

Son: E-mail, the Web – it's kind of like a giant encyclopaedia.

Mum: Why don't you use that Encyclopaedia Brittanica I bought you for Christmas?

'The secret of my success'

...or lack thereof. They clearly aren't that interested in understanding what the Internet is about, but it does aptly illustrate how difficult it is to succinctly describe in layman's terms what the Internet actually is. A global system for cultural and technical information dispersal? Not exactly jargon-free, not exactly definitive.

The other niggling little thing is that you don't want them to think you're a spotty little nerd, by describing the thing as a global community or suchlike. They might disown you, or worse pull out the phone line.

The problem is that they take the clearly ill-informed opinion of our irate news editor friend as the gospel regarding technological issues. Leaving my axe to grind for a moment, the best course of action is to *laissez faire* – leave alone. It's hard to understand how the Internet works if you haven't experienced its full breadth yourself, and nigh impossible if the person you are trying to explain it to isn't really *that* interested.

Kibo is a bit of a net legend. He got his first e-mail account in 1985, and news access in 1989, and since then certain newsgroups have never been the same again.

His real name is James Parry and he first shot to fame because he used to read every post on Usenet which had his online pseudonym in it: 'kibo'. Eventually people tried to make this quite impossible by putting his name in their signature files giving rise to a whole plethora of kibo related lunacies. Despite the huge number of hours he spent each day online, there were too many posts to respond to, so he employed the help of what became known as his 'kibological minions'.

Of course, Kibo's signatures were quite witty as well, with him and his friends professing to be famous people and 'friends of kibo'. His signature file changed his 'sig' every time he posted, so he had quite a few different ones – the daily event of every Usenetter's life. How sad does this sound?

Here are some of Kibo's more popular 'sigs'.

```
--
Bundy, Al (196, 345)

A man. A REAL Man. A Real Man's man. A Real friend of Kibo's.
```

A fairly stock, standard example. For anyone not entirely engrossed in American culture, Al Bundy is the star of 'Married With Children'.

```
--
Graber, Harry

11-Year old who is dying of a fatal disease. Want to break the world
record for most copies of Kibo's .signature file.
```

This is a rather cruel jibe at Craig Shergold, who was dying of cancer and wanted to collect as many 'get well post cards' as he could. Unfortunately most of the Net is rather fed up of Craig Shergold (who incidentally did get better) – see next net legend.

--
Voltaire (422)

French philosopher, writer, statesman, and too dead to be Kibo's friend.

Yeah, whatever!

Kibology – the religion

This rather skinny man, with a haircut like Harrison Ford and a skin tone like Michael Jackson, has net fame, even a presidential election campaign, but more still he has a religion, all of his own.

Of course, like most things on the Net, Kibology isn't something that anyone fully understands. In a serious sense it is 'doing what Kibo does'. In a distinctly less than serious sense it is a complete joke – but, let's forget that for a moment.

Kibo is by all accounts a very funny man, who appears to take nothing seriously and doesn't have a great deal of time for Internet prudery and netiquette. His idea that everyone should loosen up, chill out and have fun is a concept that should be gaining support, whether it's called Kibology or not.

What REALLY made Kibo famous?

Just being a bit witty and doing some strange things surely can't win you the following that a net icon like Kibo has achieved. True. What really shot Kibo to fame was that he invented the smiley.

This little three character hedonic symbol is something which is so commonly used on the Internet today that it seems strange to think that at one time it was never used at all. Kibo claims to have invented it, and no-one seems to dispute it – but then, you never can be sure!

Interestingly enough he also claims to be able to type the darn things in a tenth of a second, which by all accounts is pretty good going!

Craig Shergold

Anyone who ever had the misfortune to watch 'Record Breakers', with the trumpeting Roy Castle and Cheryl Baker, of Bucks Fizz fame, will surely know of Craig Shergold, who broke the world record for the most 'get well postcards' received by one person about six years ago.

At the time, e-mail letters proliferating around the Internet asked people to send the cards. Unfortunately they didn't stop, the result being that many years later, the letters still keep flooding in, and the spams keep being bandied about.

The sub post office in the little English town where Craig lives is finding the post cards a full time occupation, but the little guy did make it onto the Howard Stern show. Here is a touching example of how mangled a spam can become, especially in the hands of EFL speakers.

> I received this mail this morning and it touched my heart. Pass it on to
> friends and let's try to help him reach his goal!!
>
> Thank you!
>
> ***This is very serious***
> Craig Shergold is a 7 year old boy who lives in Keene, N.H. He is dying from an inoperable brain tumor. He made a wish to Children's Wish Foundation, that he wants one million get well cards sent to him by August 15 so he can make the world book of records before he dies, cards can be made or bought, PLEASE send the cards to the following address:

> Craig Shergold
> c/o Children Wish Foundation
> 32 Perimeter Center East
> Atlanta, Georgia 30346
>
> PLEASE pass on to churches, schools, girl scouts, boy scouts, your centers...

The only thing I can say if you get one of these things, (many of which are sent with the best of intentions) is to ignore it and inform the sender of the real state of events – oh, and, of course, tell them to buy this book...

Dave Rhodes

Around 1987 or 1988, a student by the name of Dave Rhodes transcribed a traditional postal pyramid scheme into a computer. I can't prove that was the first time it had been done electronically, but by all accounts his chain letter is the "big daddy" of them all. Millions of copies of the wretched things have traversed the Internet in the last ten years, and as we all know, human greed is boundless.

Unfortunately, human intelligence is not (boundless, that is). Therefore, not only are people still degenerate enough to send them, but some are even stupid enough to send their money off, via Her Majesty's PO.

An example of a MMF (Make Money Fast) scam, of the pyramid post variety is shown in Chapter Ten. Of course, they don't work, because even if anyone was gullible enough to fall for it, they don't have to send money to anyone on the list for the scam to make money for them.

Among his admirers is Spamford Wallace, the undisputed 'King of Spam' who now owns Cyber Promotions Inc, the company every Internet user just loves to hate. Although, Wallace's UCE advertises a product, service or site, it is no less fraudulent.

Getting back to our dear friend, Mr. Rhodes. He was a student at Columbia Union College in Takoma Park, MD, a Seventh Day Adventist college. A long time after his original misdemeanour, he apologised, but it is unknown whether or not the college disciplined him for his stupidity.

Rumour has it that he went to Federal prison for the scam – I don't know if it's true, but it should be. Anyhow wherever he may be, be it in prison (unlikely) or on a Caribbean beach sunning away his $650 zillion (more unlikely still) we'd just like him to know that millions of Net users would really like to kick his butt.

Michael Lawrie

Michael Lawrie, also known by his online handle 'Lorry', is a Commercial Security Consultant. Born in 1968, he first used Internet-esque networks, in 1982, at the age of 14, making him one of the first generations of young Internet spods.

The term 'spod' is a non-deprecating term for a geek. Recently featured in the OED, Lawrie claims he invented the word.

In 1984, Michael became responsible for running his first MUD (Multiuser Dungeon). It was written by him and a friend (Neil Burgess) and ran on a Prime 2250 at Accrington and Rossendale College.

He then progressed up the MUD admin's political ladder until eventually in 1987 he took control of one of the Essex Systems MUDs, known as MIST, and eventually by 1992 came to control most of the publicly accessible leisure activities on JANET (the UK's Joint Academic Network).

In 1991 he closed MIST down, his excuse being '*Better it was, to die in glory than rot in mediocrity*'.

He was termed by the national rags as the '*Information Superhighwayman*' for his attempt to register *http://www.harrods.com,* but Mr. Al Fayed soon got his hands on him and made him give it back – minus some compensation, or so the story goes.

He was also largely responsible for the split within EfNet, with its European elements becoming IRCnet – another one of Lawrie's online escapades.

Michael Lawrie is a strong believer in self-regulation rather than intervention. He has at brief times made sweeping entrances into Usenet (his Field of Dreams post being mildly famous and repeated in part in Chapter Seven, 'How and When to Complain'). On the whole he doesn't rate the medium, believing that anyone who has that much time to compose a response can at least make a decent job of it.

Like most Internet users, Michael just loves to be flattered and written about, and has a huge ego; but he is a bloke who exudes common sense – if more people listened to him, the Internet would surely be a better place.

Tim Berners-Lee

Tim Berners-Lee is a man known to most as 'the Father of the World Wide Web'. He graduated from Queen's College, Oxford, in 1976. Whilst there he built his first computer with a soldering iron, TTL gates, an M6800 processor and an old TV set.

Thirteen years later, he proposed a global hypertext project, to be known as the World Wide Web. Based on the earlier 'Enquire' work, it was designed to allow people to work together remotely by combining their knowledge in a web of hypertext documents.

He wrote the first World Wide Web server and the first client, a primitive hypertext browser/editor which ran in the NeXTStep environment. This work was started in October 1990, and the program 'WorldWideWeb' first made available within CERN in December, and on the Internet at large in the summer of 1991.

Tim continued to work on his brainchild, receiving feedback from users within CERN and the growing Internet as a whole. Meanwhile he developed and enhanced the specifications for web addressing and HTML – the scripting language behind the World Wide Web.

In 1994, Berners-Lee joined the Laboratory for Computer Science (LCS) at the Massachusetts Institute of Technology. He was to head up a W3C consortium to maintain and agree standards for HTTP, (Hypertext Transfer Protocol – the exchange of information from web server to client) HTML (Hypertext Markup Language – the script which web pages are written in) and other WWW related protocols.

In 1995, he won the Kilby Foundation's 'Young Innovator of the Year' Award, whilst in 1996 he received the IEEE Computer Society Wallace McDowell Award, and was co-recipient of the Computers and Communication Prize. He was also graced with various honorary degrees, including a doctorate from the University of Southampton. A *pater patria* of the online world, in a hundred years time he may be viewed as one of the most notable men of the 20th Century.

Vint Cerf

Universally heralded as the great granddaddy of the Internet, Vint Cerf is another one of those names you really shouldn't forget. Currently Senior VP of Internet Architecture and Engineering at MCI Communications, it was he and Robert Kahn who gave the first spark of life to decentralised computer networks when they devised the TCP/IP protocol suite at the same time as they were sending men to the moon. In December 1997, President Bill Clinton awarded both of them the US National Medal of Technology for their work.

His role as a founding father was again pivotal during his tenure at DARPA (Defence's Advanced Research Project Agency) from 1976 until 1982.

Cerf served as founding president of the Internet Society from 1992–1995. He is a fellow of the IEEE, ACM, and American Association for the Advancement of Science, the American Academy of Arts and Sciences and the National Academy of Engineering.

The Internet Society is a non-profit, non-governmental, international, professional membership organisation. It focuses on standards, education, and policy issues. Comprised of more than 100 organisational and 6,000 individual members worldwide, it represents a veritable 'who's who' of the Internet community.

Cerf holds numerous degrees: a bachelors in Mathematics from Stanford University together with an MSc and a PhD from UCLA. In addition to this he also holds an honorary Doctorate degree in Science and Maths from the University of Balearic Isles. Lectures on the beach – hmmm...

His public image isn't perhaps as altruistic as Berners-Lee's, although that's probably more to do with Cerf's commercial orientation – Berners-Lee is quite firmly rooted in academia. However, without Vint Cerf's work there probably would be no Internet ... and no World Wide Web either. He's also the author of a concise and undoubtedly accurate history of the Internet – see page 185 for details of this publication.

Jarkko Oikarinen

Internet Relay Chat was Jarkko Oikarinen's brainchild, whilst supposedly working (although by his account, actually doing very little) at the Department of Information Processing Science at the University of Oulu, Finland, in 1988. He began work on a communications program to add Usenet-esque as well as real-time functionality to Oulubox, a Finnish BBS system.

There were already a few systems in place on the BBS, MUT (Multi-user Talker) and 'rmsg' being two examples. The latter, closely derived from the UNIX facility 'talk', did not have support for channels, whilst the former was unstable and buggy.

Oikarinen admits that much of the inspiration for IRC came from Bitnet Relay Chat – a very different client and server set up, however.

The first IRC client and server was finally completed in August 1988, the first server being *tolsun.oulu.fi,* in Northern Finland. As it grew in popularity and started to get two figure concurrent connections, another server was set up in Southern Finland.

Internet connectivity to the Finnish networks was very limited, so it took a while for IRC to catch on. Nowadays, hundreds of thousands of people use IRC every day.

In an interview with the Undernet Public Relations Committee, Oikarinen remarked: '*There are scalability problems with IRC. I never imagined that it would be quite this popular. The main problem is with nicknames. Although there are almost 5 billion permutations of the 9 character series, they aren't all desirable or easily identifiable.*'

Since 1990, Oikarinen has had very little to do with the development of the IRC protocols (RFC1459). He doesn't expect to have much input into them in the future either: '*...right now I am working towards my PhD and it really consumes all my time. I will be listening but not actively participating...*'

Khaled Mardam-Bey

Continuing on the IRC theme, Mardam-Bey is the writer of the Internet's most popular IRC client, mIRC. It added extra, if proprietary, functionality to the IRC experience, with coloured text using control codes as well as support for sound. On a more pragmatic note it also supports DCC (Direct Client-to-Client) Chat, which enables you to conduct stable private conversations and DCC File Transfer which lets you exchange files readily between users.

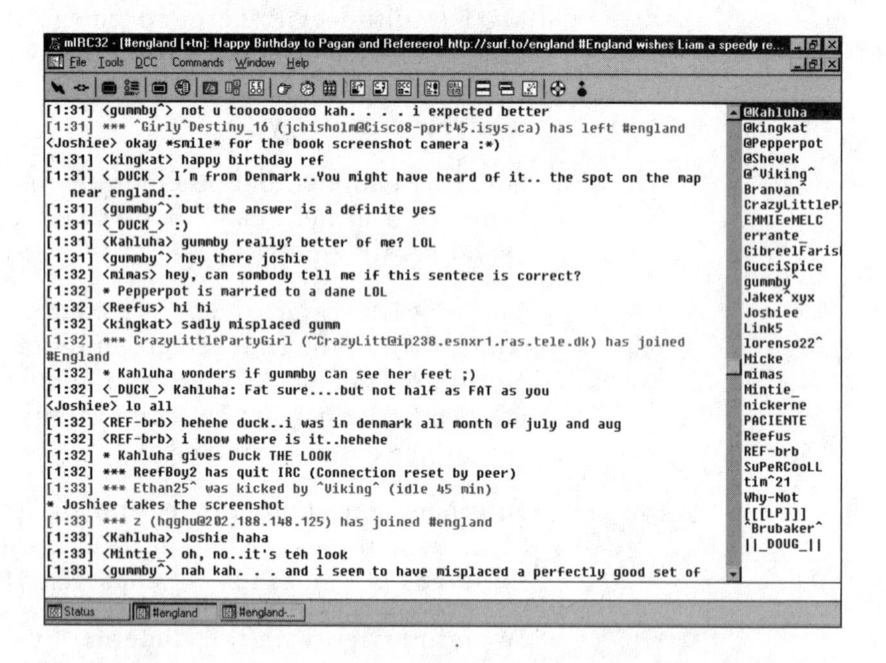

Shareware programs enable you to trial software for a limited period before deciding whether to pay for it.

The writer is famous because a rather geekish picture of him appears each time you launch the program. He was born in Amman, Jordan, in 1968, the son of a Syrian Father and a Palestinian Mother.

He studied at the American University in Washington DC, from which he graduated with a BSc in Information Systems. He is now a Cognitive Science graduate student at the University of Westminster. He seems to think that the best thing about London is the 'spiffy red buses' and sees IRC as the way forward to social enlightenment.

The mIRC program was originally a freeware project, but in order to finance its continuing development he's now requesting a £10 or $20 registration fee for the shareware version.

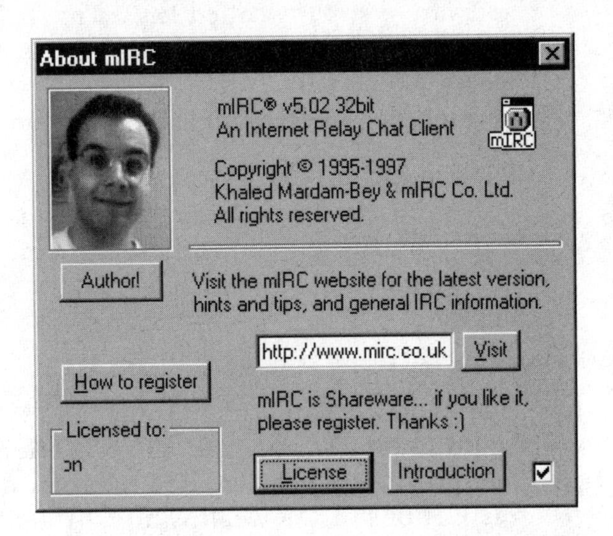

You may find that many Internet old-timers object to proprietary programs like mIRC. The control characters used to indicate colour just litter displays with rubbish in older UNIX clients, and the popups create a text kludge.

Mardam-Bey is a strong believer in social activism, and tends to suggest that his motives for writing the mIRC program, now with over a hundred thousand users, were altruistic rather than commercial. Considering the limited financial success of shareware software this seems quite probable.

His main interests are now his Jasmine tree (his Bonsai tree apparently died), origami, meditating with the help of his bedroom wall and doing lots of other really strange and wacky things.

The self designated part-time Human Bean has been working on mIRC for three years and does intend to continue his work, the latest version of which is available from the mIRC web site.

Hook up your phone and waggle your browser at *http://www.mirc.co.uk.*

Cliff Stanford

Cliff was born in 1954 and in 1972 began training as a chartered accountant. By 1979 he had set up his first software company called ImPETus, that developed software for the Commodore PET machines. After the PET computer began to die, Cliff started Demon Systems as a company developing MS-DOS and UNIX systems.

Back in the dark and dank days of 1992, Cliff Stanford posted an article to Usenet asking for £120. There wasn't much to distinguish his message from the other commercial spams, which were, at the time, few and far between.

He launched a service, initially hoping to be merely self financing to enable FTP, Telnet and e-mail access to the Internet for £12 a month. He was offering a service which had previously been limited to large corporations, academic institutions or the wealthy and affluent.

Demon Internet therefore began more as a club for friends and colleagues to gain access to the Internet and was the first company to use its name in e-mail addresses. It started with 200 subscribers, eight modems, a few phone lines and an Internet feed from Pipex.

Stanford's initial ambition was to hook up 200 members in the first year. As Demon Internet was merely a sideline to Demon Internet Systems the company accounts were even being run out of the back of Stanford's Mum's kitchen diary. By word of mouth the company steadily grew and by the end of the first year of operation had far superseded Stanford's initial goal. Forecasts for the company had estimated 400 subscribers in 6 months, 1,000 in 2 years and 4,500 users by October 1995 – less than three years after the company started. In actual fact, by October 1995 Demon Internet was running a service for 45,000 subscribers.

Now the company goes on, with Stanford having sold out to Scottish Telecom for the sum of £33 million. This is invested in his latest venture, Redbus – a management firm aiding new technology companies. One to watch!

Chapter Twelve

The Last Word

This is the chapter which ties up all the proverbial loose ends, tells you all the stuff you *really* ought to know and where to look if you want to know more.

Covers

The Future of the Internet

Predicting the future is a practice treated harshly by posterity. In the unlikely event you get it right, few people appreciate it as being anything other than obvious. If you get it wrong, which is more than likely, you get shunned and ridiculed – chin rubbing all around.

Online evolution

Few things on the Internet stay the same for very long, being the volatile, almost organic system that it is. Instantaneous media (such as IRC) are undoubtedly going to change from being primarily text based to a more visual and aural experience, through the use of video and sound.

Usenet, e-mail and other non-interactive communicative devices may become less popular (or grow slowly in comparison to other services) just in the same way as the interactivity of the telephone has reduced the art of letter writing to mere business correspondence.

It is also likely that the Internet will develop many more commercial outlets. As well as allowing businesses to transfer information more effectively, the potential for retailing will inevitably become the 'buzz thing' for the next millennium. Clearly, Nostradamus didn't predict Armageddon coming in the form of an online McDonalds.

One undeniably excellent thing is that the Net will get quicker. We have already seen cable modems, new fibre optic technology and satellite links able to boost the speed a hundredfold of not only data communications at the user's end, but in the trunk lines which connect ISPs to ISPs, and continents to continents. I doubt we'll have to wait long for all this to come together and manifest itself in the information infrastructure.

Technological convergence

What we may also experience is a convergence between the Internet and other information services. In the future, TV will not only run along the same cables as the telecommunications network, but will be virtually unidentifiable from it. Television will sport interactivity, whilst the Internet will offer the quality of prepared programming that was previously only the domain of the blessed telly.

Functionality

The eventual transition of mainstream services towards the Internet will inevitably require greater functionality than was offered by their previous forms. Development responds to demand, so an Internet terminal should be cheaper than a TV, portable like a newspaper (ie, so you can read it in the bath – come to think of it, waterproof would be good as well) and offer something more – interaction and choice.

Education

Sky Television tried to justify their exorbitantly high subscription costs by describing the television as the *'greatest education resource of the 20th Century'*. Yeah, right – I'm sure the Simpsons would agree!

It is commonly recognised that everyone learns differently, but also that most people benefit from a 'pro-active' educational experience, which is what the Internet can offer over the passive content of a television network.

You could have a video lesson take place and then a short test could be given to examine the student's comprehension of the subject. This two way medium also enables feedback to be given and help to be offered in return.

It is unlikely that this kind of teaching could replace conventional pedagoguery entirely, although it could be integrated into a conventional scheme. The main problem lies perhaps in a younger person's (and I generalise here!) usual lack of self-discipline when it comes to home study. It would, however, be an invaluable contribution towards adult education programmes.

Imagining society is part of creating it, and limits to imagination are also limits for creation. Those who realise this will know best what the future holds for the Internet or conversely what the Internet holds for the future.

The indistinguishable Internet

Today, a large majority of people talk about the Net as though it is some mysterious creature; an interesting novelty and a rather peculiar concept that isn't really a part of everyday life. They might fling web addresses from advertisements and e-mail addresses on business cards, but it is quite easy to imagine a world without it.

In the 'here and now' the Internet is useful, but it is essentially a hobby, a pastime and, most of all, an experience. In the future it will seem to be a practical tool, and a necessary convenience. Just like a telephone or a microwave, although you could probably do without them, they are in nearly every home, and most people use them every day.

The road behind?

When the Net loses its identity as a separate entity and its individualism, it will inevitably lose its individual culture as well. No doubt, future netizens will find the mystique and culture of the present day Internet a distinguishing mark of our era.

There aren't many cases in the history of man where interpersonal contact has taken a truly bizarre turn. For thousands of years there have been wars, conflicts, writing and oratory, but never in the past, and probably never in the future, will there ever be anything like the Internet.

Television couch potatoes everywhere are bombarded by the hyperbole-rich advertisements of telecommunications companies, but Orange in particular has struck a chord with me.

To paraphrase:

'In the future the Internet will become our lives: working without leaving your desk, without meeting people. In the future, woman will not meet man, and man will not meet woman ... Not in our future.'

Addicted to Bits

The Internet is like a drug, and can be addictive. It's quite scary when you go on holiday for two weeks, and after two days feel the sudden pang to check your e-mail. The day before you return home, you have nightmares about how you're going to read all the posts in *demon.service* and still manage to get to work in the morning.

Of course, it's not physically compulsive like cigarettes or other addictive drugs, but not using the Internet is like falling out with your best friend – there's a huge gap in your life.

I'm not saying that I couldn't throw my modem out of the window, my keyboard in the bin and never surf the Net or weave the Web again (after 180-odd pages that's exactly what I feel like doing). To employ another analogy, it's rather like playing the guitar: if it sits in the corner of the room, you just can't resist picking it up and playing it.

If you go to someone's house and see a shiny beeping box on top of their PC you just can't resist quizzing them intimately on the state of their online presence. Have they got a web page? What's their e-mail address? What do they think of ISP XYZ?

Worse still the impulse is there to sit down and have a fiddle, and in typical Netesque style, educate them, belittle them and impress upon them your expert technical knowledge.

The social dilemma

On the Internet, the art of baffling and 'techy talk' is one that is highly regarded, yet in real life the reverse is certainly true. People often show disinterest and contempt for anything they cannot, or do not, understand.

There are few things in the field of general human understanding as poorly understood as the Internet – although neurology and the contents of McDonald's beefburgers come a close second.

For this reason, much as it is against their nature, most netizens would never raise the subject of online communications in a real life conversation. The social disdain would be too great and the misconceptions too irritating to even begin to remedy. The general perception of the Internet, as a cross between a shopping mall and a newsagent's top shelf, really rubs the average netizen up the wrong way.

On the off chance that the Internet oracle in question is levelled with enthusiasm at the prospect of explaining what it is like, there are other problems. For example, it is very easy to describe a holiday location like Disneyland and why you went there, because they are physical places, with some very definable qualities or characteristics. Imagine, however, trying to describe the Internet – what it is, what it does, what it's like. In some respects, it's an elaborate telephone, in others it is like a huge encyclopaedia and maybe in yet another it is merely a convenience and an expense – rather like the QVC shopping channel.

When we describe what something is like, we tend to do so in relations to things both we and the listener know well. For example, we could say that Disneyland is like Alton Towers, but bigger and better and that the Golden Gate bridge is like the Severn bridge on stilts.

The problem is that because the Internet is so bizarrely unique we have no reference with which to describe it. Therefore, the only way to really understand the Internet is to use it and experience it. As the proverb says: *'I can explain it for you, but I can't understand it for you.'*

A moment's ponder

When I first started out on Usenet I remember posting an article to a newsgroup called *claranet.local* – it was a general chat group for users of the ISP, ClaraNet. It was a wee little tale of how people often found computers difficult to understand. I remember firing up my newsreader, first of all twice a day, and then on the second day I would do it once every two hours, and then once an hour, until eventually I was sat at my PC for a whole evening, randomly flicking between Web pages and desperately waiting for a response. I suppose what I really wanted was recognition. My post was like a shrill call, *'hey look over here – can you see me?'* There are many things that irritate people, like being insulted, or being scoffed at, but worst of all is being ignored.

Need I say it: no-one replied to my post. A day, a week, a month and then my post passed into oblivion and, finally, the expiration bin. What I realise now is that I wasn't really interested in making a contribution to the Network or giving something to everyone else – be it wit, humour or information. All I really wanted was someone to see I was there. My post was selfish, self-centred and got the lack of attention that it deserved.

Net death

There is a time when, after a long session of Net surfing (usually in the early morning hours when you're overdosed on caffeine, underdosed on sleep and your fingers ache like crazy) you want to do nothing more than flip the clunky little power switch on your PC and bask in a sea of eternal nothingness. But you can't.

You sit there, a huge store of information at your fingertips, almost everything you ever wanted to know just a few mouse clicks away, but you just aren't interested anymore. You don't care for that riveting bit of trivia on how snakes copulate, nor that terribly funny joke about Bill Gates. All you want to do is exist in a state of communication limbo, trying to get away from the voices in your head.

It may sound like the ravings of a mad-man, but sometimes the voices of every Usenet poster you've read, every IRCer you've talked to and the author of every Web page you've browsed reaches out to you and tries to communicate with you. The information flings itself at you, but you cannot absorb any of it. It is relentless, annoying and very, very strange!

Identifying Addiction

It's difficult to tell when someone is truly addicted to the Internet, particularly when the potential addict is yourself. Besides which, I wouldn't worry, there are many more less productive pastimes. Well ... actually, not that many – tiddlywinks, jigsaws and maybe politics as well.

Symptoms

There follows some excellent 'top tips' for you to try, and common symptoms to identify this affliction. I'm still working on the cure, but don't worry, it'll be in the next edition. Promise.

From the top, ten ways to tell that you're spending *too long* online:

1. When someone tells a joke you shout 'L-O-L' across the room.
2. You find yourself cocking your head 90 degrees to the right when trying to smile.
3. Your spouse complains about you moving your fingertips whilst trying to conduct a normal conversation.
4. When people ask *'What did you say?'* you reply, *'Scroll up!'*
5. You know more about your IRC friends' daily routines than you do about your own family.
6. You go into labour and you stop to type a special E-mail to let everyone know you're going to be away and how you're feeling.
7. You meet someone who you hate in real life and look for the ignore button.
8. You abandon the English language in favour of a more abbreviated form. You drop words like *'bbl,' 'rtfm,'* and *'re'* into your communiques and no-one can understand a word you're saying.

9. You can actually read and follow the credits at the end of a film.
10. You double-click your TV remote.
11. Your greatest chat-up line is *'a-s-l?'*
12. You wake up at four in the morning to go to the toilet, but then check your e-mail first.
13. Your last 'sexual' experience was really just a 'textual' experience.
14. You know what a 'BIFF' is.
15. You think the most topical source of news on the planet is *misc.misc.*
16. When seeing someone you wish to meet, your second thought is wishing they were on IRC so you don't have to meet them in person.
17. You're actually laughing at these jokes.

On a serious note

Addiction can be a problem. Combined with the online experience, it's the stuff that falling grades, a failing social life and missed book deadlines (personal experience) are made of.

If you want to cut down your time online, try to set rules on a daily basis for the time you spend hogging the phone line. The Internet isn't a full substitute for seeing the real world, once in a while. Getting out and seeing your 'real life' friends is a good idea. Just as sometimes you escape real life by hooking up your modem, sometimes you want to escape the Internet by hooking into real life. If that day comes, you really will need a life to go back to.

Pearls of Digital Wisdom

I am but one person amongst millions on the Internet, yet as far as your understanding of the online world goes, I'm probably the loudest voice ringing in your head. Rather than let that be the case, I've compiled a list of sayings by famous and authoritative Internet propeller heads, cluebies and influential netizens for your personal perusal:

'I stop where a wet walkway meets a dry one and stand for a sec, look down at my soggy moccasins, and start thinking about this thing *that buzzes around the entire world, through the phone lines, all day and all night long. It's right under our noses and it's invisible. It's like Narnia, or Magritte, or Star Trek, an entire goddamned world. Except it doesn't physically exist. It's just the collective consciousness of however many people are on it. This is outstandingly weird.'*

JC Herz, *Surfing on the Internet*
(ISBN 0-349-10773-4)

'For a technologist, the future is rosy; for private citizens and those who can trade or work over the Internet, it is probably equally rosy, but with a few difficult aspects. But for many the Cybernation presents a challenging picture. Tomorrow's challenge to today is one we must *face today; by the time tomorrow comes it may be too late.'*

N Barrett, *State of the Cybernation*
(ISBN 0-7494-2054-5)

'I think this is a wonderful time to be alive. There have never been so many opportunities to do things that were impossible before ... The information highway will lead to many destinations, and the Internet is the 'The Road Ahead'. In any case, I'm excited to be on the journey.'

Bill Gates, *The Road Ahead*
(ISBN 0-670-77289-5)

'IRC, just like the Internet itself, is a beautiful and immensely empowering and important tool that will change the way humans know each other.'

Khaled Mardam-Bey, *Author of mIRC*

'The notion that the Internet is mostly about sex is nonsense. The vast majority of our customers have little or no interest in it.'

Steve Case, *founder and chairman of AOL*

'One thing is certain. The Web will have a profound effect on the markets and the cultures around the world: intelligent agents will either stabilise or destabilise markets; the demise of distance will either homogenise or polarise cultures; the ability to access the Web will be either a great divider or a great equaliser; the path will either lead to jealousy and hatred or peace and understanding.'

Tim Berners-Lee, *Father of the World Wide Web*

'Three months after I joined, I went to my first WELL party at the home of one of the WELL's online moderators. I looked around at the room full of strangers when I walked in. It was one of the oddest sensations of my life. I had contended with these people, shot the invisible breeze round the electronic watercooler, shared alliances and formed bonds, fallen off my chair laughing with them. There wasn't a recognizable face in the house.'

Howard Rheingold, *The Virtual Community*

And now for the clangers...

'As we connect every school and classroom to the Internet, we must protect our children from the red-light districts of cyberspace.'

Al Gore, *US Vice President*

'It (the Internet) has become a monstrous vehicle, and at the moment decent people are impotent to curb the evil that is being perpetrated.'

Lynda Lee-Potter, *Daily Mail*

And a famous fellow with foresight...

'This Encyclopaedic organization need not be concentrated now in one place; it might have the form of a network. It would centralize mentally but perhaps not physically.'

H. G. Wells, *World Brain*

Useful Sites

If you are prepared to seek, you shall find. There is an abundance of Web sites offering helpful hints on how to negotiate all the tricky values, codes of conduct and behaviour that prevail on the Internet.

'The Road Ahead' by Bill Gates is one book you really should read. It is (as you would expect) heavily oriented towards the commercial applications of the Internet, but nevertheless it is a seminal work.

- **Cyber 24:** *http://www.cyber24.com*

  This site really rocks. Very hip and very modern it gives an altogether original and photographic account of the lives of thousands of digital revolutionaries during a 24 hour period. Quite stunning, quite amazing, and available in traditional 'pen and pulp' paperback as well.

- **The Jargon File 4.0.0:** *http://earthspace.net/jargon/*

  The Jargon File is the most comprehensive 'hackeresque' lexicon of the online *lingua franca* available. Originally started in the 1970s and 80s to help new users get to grips with the jargon, much of the material it contains is deeply rooted in technicalia.

- **FAQs:** *http://www.faqs.org*

  A vast number of Frequently Asked Questions are linked and stored here. Note the rather snazzy search facilities that make digging up stuff so much easier.

- **RTFM FTP Site:** *ftp://rtfm.mit.edu/pub/usenet/*

  This site is solely concerned with archiving FAQs which are relevant to specific newsgroups, as opposed to general subject documents. Most newsgroups have a directory; in the directories are the relevant files. As they are in alphabetical order, you just scroll down the list; alternatively, use the 'Edit-Find' option in your browser and click, click – voila!

- **WIRED News:** *http://www.wired.com*

  This site is conclusive proof that looks can be deceiving. The graphics may look like they come from the bitty display of a Spectrum 48k, but the content is just fab and regularly updated. The excellent editorial style makes for a thoroughly enjoyable and informative read on topical technological issues.

- **A Primer on How to Work with the Usenet Community:** *http://www.lib.ox.ac.uk/internet/news/faq/archive/usenet.primer.part1.html*

  This is the seminal guide to Netiquette written by Chuq von Rospach. The ultimate in prudish pernicketying, it is worth reading. If you think it's sagely or if you disagree, at least you'll know what you're up against.

- **Dejanews:** *http://www.dejanews.com*

  An invaluable news archive site, with records going back over five years. Whether you're looking for ammo for a flame fest or just topical research, this is about as organised as chaotic NetNews gets.

- **Brief History of the Internet and Related Networks:** *http://www.simmons.edu/~pomerant/techcomp/cerf.html*

  Written by Vint Cerf, the man commonly regarded as the Father of the Internet (see Chapter Eleven), this site can only be described (despite its many weaknesses) as authoritative – a 'must read', straight from the horse's mouth.

- **Short History of the World Wide Web:** *http://www.w3.org/People/Berners-Lee/ShortHistory.html*

  In the same way that Cerf provides a definitive account of the Internet, Tim Berners-Lee (see Chapter Eleven) does the same for the World Wide Web. Extremely well written, it clearly explains not only how the Web was developed, but why it developed in the way it did.

- **'The Virtual Community' Online by Howard Rheingold:** *http://www.rheingold.com*

  The Internet Culture book that most people believe to be seminal. Rheingold thinks that if data communications is not 'pushed' it will pass like a fad and not become part of the political and social systems in the way that many netizens envisage. He talks about questioning the reality of the 'online culture', segregating it from what is 'real life culture' – but although they are different blossoms, they both come from the same flower.

The Internet and Real Life

I've tried not to rant in this book. Once you get beyond those irresistible little analogies which are the salvation of every second rate technology writer – 'IRC is like CB radio,' 'The Internet is like a giant encyclopaedia' amongst other inane cliches, you have a problem. There are usually two courses of action.

You either try to delve into your personal experiences, in which case no-one who isn't a verified propeller head can understand a word you're saying, or you write lots of journalese-style hyperbole, seasoned with rip offs from online sources. It's the choice between preaching to the converted or saying what people expect to hear, however untrue that may be.

I've tried to take another road, but here is my little ditty at the end, where I waffle on about my latest bug bears and gripes, thoughts, experiences and exercise an overly vivid imagination – just like everyone else.

Are you sitting comfortably? Then we'll begin...

What I've written about is 'my' experience of the Internet – indeed, I don't think I could do anything else. The point is, although I may be qualified to write about the 'dreaming spires of Oxford' (I live there) I'm not exactly an authority on the mating habits of Zulu maidens. I'm not a Zulu and I've never been to South Africa – I have watched the film though...

Of course, you wouldn't expect me to write a travel article without having any personal experience of an area, yet strangely enough this is something that is common in technology writing. The Internet is a big place.

You cannot define this 'network of networks' in a sentence, a page, a chapter or even a book. It's like a virtual country. Although its many different parts have certain areas of commonality, you can't define IRC in the same way as Usenet any more than you could say that Johannesburg is the same as Cape Town or LA is the same as San Francisco.

To understand the Internet fully you have to understand the people who use it, because it means something different to everyone. Sure, I think San Francisco is a fantastic place, but the ex-inhabitants of Alcatraz probably disagree.

Needless to say, not many people who compulsively use the Internet actually 'hate it' else they wouldn't spend their days tippy tapping away at it.

Real Life?

Many things on the Internet are analogous to real life events and experiences. Of course, it's not all to do with superhighways and communities. To see what the Internet really 'means', remembering of course that it means something different to everyone, requires omniscience – the ability to delve into everyone's minds.

I can see these parallels, but then I realise that they aren't parallels at all. Most netizens spend a lot of time defining their activities into 'real life stuff' and 'Internet stuff'. It's wrong.

Despite being only mere mortals, we should realise that these aren't two separate worlds, they're the same world and the Internet is just a bunch of routers, switchers and millions of miles of cable.

The Internet IS part of real life and it's here to stay. The people who you type to on the Internet aren't really any different to those you speak to every day of the week. What it does offer, however, is a means by which people can communicate in not only a much more efficient, but for now at least, a much more personal way. I would say categorically that this is its greatest benefit.

All Good Things....

Well, this is the end. The last page, the final word of sagely advice, the conclusion to the epic. Modesty abounds.

I have no doubt that people will look back in 50 years time and see the birth and growth of the Internet as the pivot of the technological revolution. Why do I think this? What is really special and unique about the Net is that it is one of those rare moments in history where technological advancement aids cultural development. Within the last 200 years, stages of technological progression seem 'ten-a-penny'. From the light bulb, to the telephone, to the calculator and to the computer. I think the Internet is another peak in this wave. I'm not saying that I think it's going to make this wave of development stop, but it has, and will continue to change, the way the world works.

Although it may all have started back in a small lab, thirty years ago, the most radical changes, not in terms of technology, but in terms of magnitude have happened within the last three or four years and are still happening today. It is an incredibly exciting time for technologists – the emergence of a tremendous new scientific achievement to break into the mainstream.

Use it, enjoy it and remember it. I remember my Grandmother telling me what it was like to live in a world without any TV sets, or radios. A world yet to face huge social developments and upheavals. She said although it seemed slightly primitive, it had a kind of culture that she thought we had lost or changed – a kind of culture that she missed.

In another 50 years, I will probably look back and say, 'It was a very different place. The early Internet was not a part of real life, it was special, almost mysterious.' What will you say?

We live in exciting times, and I for one intend to be a part of them.

Index